ATTENTION DEFICIT DISORDER IN ADULTS

Dr. Lynn Weiss

Foreword by
Kenneth A. Bonnet, Ph.D.

TAYLOR PUBLISHING COMPANY
DALLAS, TEXAS

Also by Lynn Weiss

Power Lines
(with Lora Cain)

I Wasn't Finished With Life
(with Dorothy and Judy Thatch)

Freedom To Joy
(with Angie Rose)

Emotionally Yours

Designed by Deborah Jackson-Jones

Published by Taylor Publishing Company
              1550 West Mockingbird Lane
              Dallas, Texas 75235

Library of Congress Cataloging-in-Publication Data

Weiss, Lynn.
      Attention deficit disorder in adults / Lynn Weiss.
          p.   cm.
      Includes bibliographical references.
      ISBN 0-87833-779-2 : $19.95 — ISBN 0-87833-782-2 : $12.95
      1. Attention-deficit hyperactivity disorder—Popular works.
      2. Attention-deficit hyperactivity disorder—Age factors.
      I. Title.
      RJ506.H9W445   1991
      616.85'89—dc20   91-28710
                                                        CIP

Printed in the United States of America
FIFTEENTH PRINTING

Acknowledgments

▼

A big special thanks goes to my son, Mendel, who initially brought ADD to my attention as an eight-year-old child. He taught me to parent differently, and he motivated me to find out all that I could about ADD so he could have a good life.

Thanks to Aaron, my older son, who became an advocate for his brother and helped us understand what it's like to be a sibling of someone with ADD.

Dale Cheney, who helped with the writing of this project and who has become a good friend, deserves special acknowledgment. He learned more about ADD in adults than he may have ever dreamed existed and helped me arrange, condense, and write the many experiences that make up this book.

And thanks to Lora Cain, friend, colleague, and fan, who recognized that she had ADD from listening to me talk about it on the radio. Lora's generous input enriched this book immeasurably.

It is with appreciation that I acknowledge Mary Kelly, my editor, from whom I continue to learn each time we work. Her belief in the subject made this book possible.

A great big hug and sweet smile to all the people who have touched my life who have ADD as adults. This book is for you.

CONTENTS

Foreword

▼

*T*he symptoms of Attention Deficit Disorder are compromising to the individual, and to the family and persons who work with that person. Attention Deficit Disorder is also a problem to the professionals asked to deal with it, and to the professional committees asked to establish diagnostic definitions and criteria. A large number of professionals are pressed by the individual client to diagnose and treat the problem, but there is little professional training to deal with the realities of the disorders and symptoms that are collectively referred to as Attention Deficit Disorder or ADD, or ADHD (Attention Deficit Hyperactive Disorder), or ADD Residual Type. The narrow focus so often brought to bear on the individual with symptoms is that it only occurs in males, that they will outgrow it, and that Ritalin is the treatment of choice if treatment is to be undertaken. Methods of dealing with such symptoms currently include "time out," reprimanding, or stating that the individual with symptoms "needs to learn to . . ."; all are attempts to somehow coerce that person into "compliance."

The majority of symptoms subsumed under the concept of Attention Deficit Disorder are approached in the medical, psychological, educational, and family arenas with a very minimum of information about attention, attention focus, its anatomy, its mechanisms, its brain biochemical regulation, and its interaction with environmental conditions. This minimal

1

information is currently still reflected in nearly all aspects of the professional and parenting spheres, and more detailed information is often familiar only to the academician who has the least contact with the treatment or diagnosis of individuals with Attention Deficit Disorder.

Individuals with Attention Deficit Disorder may or may not also show hyperactive behaviors. They may or may not be male. Their disorder may or may not be evident to those around them. Some may simply miss bits and pieces of information presented to them that are assimilated in total by their peers in the same situation. The electrical, biochemical, anatomical, and developmental characteristics of the constellation of symptoms called Attention Deficit Disorder are now recognized as involving the central nervous system. An initiative developed by the Learning Disabilities Association of America resulted, two years later, in the report of the Interagency Committee on Learning Disabilities to the United States Congress in 1987. For the first time in Federal language, the central nervous system is seen as having a major role in these symptoms.

The book you are about to read is for the nonprofessional individual. It is intended to provide the persons with ADD and those close to them with an understanding of the symptoms and their range and diversity. Dr. Lynn Weiss has accomplished this in an unusually effective manner. But she has also accomplished the accumulation of symptoms and means of dealing with them in a manner that can be very instructive to the professional who may otherwise rely on minimal information (unless he has personally lived with, or been very close to, an individual with Attention Deficit Disorder). Dr. Weiss provides personal vignettes that allow us to understand the daily manifestations and consequences of these symptoms. Reading these personal situations takes one far away from the simplistic views that an ADD person is a young boy running erratically around a classroom, symptomatic because he is "allergic" to one food chemical or another; that ADD is definitely/definitely not to be treated with Ritalin; and that ADD sufferers definitely "outgrow"

2

their symptoms. These stereotypes slip away as one reads the professional and personal information throughout this book.

The reader quickly comes to realize the full consequences of problems with being able to maintain voluntarily focused attention on a task or situation in a systematic and sequential way. These problems with attention may or may not be made worse by certain chemicals or foodstuffs (individual sensitivities can be severe), and they may or may not be accompanied by other symptoms (including hyperactivity). For the professional, it becomes very clear that ADD/ADHD is not a singular disorder, and it does not fit existing diagnostic criteria in a large number of cases. We must begin to take each of these symptoms seriously in the perspective of small but compromising deficits in attentional mechanisms rather than labeling them with an acronym "ADD" that conjures up a reflexive and singular treatment choice.

This book should be required reading for families, friends, and individuals with Attention Deficit Disorder(s) who are inserted into the human functioning of personal space and work place. It is also recommended as reading that may very well broaden the understanding for the caring medical, psychological, or other professional who has not had the experience of living with the full ramifications of this cluster of symptoms. In the end, the caring individual can improve his understanding of the person with symptoms and through understanding can reduce the stress he experiences in trying to interact with symptoms that are not easily grasped nor fully understood.

Kenneth A. Bonnet, Ph.D.
New York, New York
August 1991

Introduction

▼

I wish I had known twenty years ago what I know now. My expectations of my son and my husband would have been much different and more realistic.

When my son's fourth grade teacher told me, "He could do his work, if he'd just settle down," I began to realize that Attention Deficit Disorder was present in my family. Sadly, I didn't do much about it then. I didn't know what to do. Besides, I thought, as most other psychotherapists and mental health professionals did then, that it would disappear when my son reached puberty.

It wasn't until my son was thirteen that my eyes were opened and I understood that ADD was a lifelong condition. My son's inability to block out the high level of activity in junior high caused him to become a frequent visitor to the principal's office. And he began to do poorly in math, the subject he had always done well at, because he couldn't concentrate on all the steps involved. I had him thoroughly evaluated for ADD and discovered he wasn't outgrowing it. In fact, far from disappearing, as we had expected it to, it was causing him more trouble, not less. And during the course of my son's evaluation, his father, by then my ex-husband, was evaluated as having it, too. It was then that I realized how ADD shapes personality, torments its victims, and fragments relationships.

At about the same time that I learned about my son and his father, two of my adult clinical psychotherapy patients failed to respond to treatment and I noticed attentional problems similar to those present in school children. When I went to the professional literature hoping to find alternative treatment for them, I discovered an article entitled, "The Diagnosis and Treatment of Attention Deficit Disorder, Residual Type," by David Woods, M.D., *Psychiatric Annals*, 16:1, January 1986, that outlined the condition in adults.

Then, on my radio talk show at KLIF in Dallas, Texas, I mentioned ADD-RT (Residual Type) and its characteristics. I watched as the phone lines lit up instantly and the switchboard accumulated a record number of requests for further information. I soon found myself deluged with requests for information about ADD in adults.

But I had very little information to offer. In my research I'd discovered there was precious little available, and what was available was scientifically oriented and not helpful to the general public.

So I developed screening procedures, seminars, workshops, and group educational/counseling sessions. An announcement to the general public of any of these opportunities met with such enthusiastic response that all the available space was immediately filled. I was impressed with how eager those who have ADD-RT and their family members were to get help.

The emotional pain of adult ADD sufferers became obvious immediately. But so too did their interest in doing something about their condition. I began to hear the same stories over and over. And they sounded all too familiar. They were *my* family's story, too. Like termites that are unseen until the very structure of the building is jeopardized, ADD undermines the abilities and personality of the individual. Its damage spreads to the relationships that are an inevitable part of each person's life. And the pain is enormous. That's why there is such a need to raise awareness of this hidden disorder that, at least in part, can be held responsible for the way many people are. And that's why there's a need to develop materials and techniques to assist in circumventing the effects of ADD in adulthood.

My own son was placed on medication and given assistance in managing his ADD and at the end of the year won the citizenship award for most improved behavior. He passed algebra, too. And now with thoughtful, skillful help, he can continue to be a happy, successful person who understands himself and his limitations and can work around them.

My intent for the readers of this book is to provide each with the same hope and opportunity for a happy, successful life despite the presence of ADD.

I have made no attempt to be inclusive. Rather, I am sharing what I have discovered works with the many hundreds of adult ADD sufferers whom I have treated over the last two years. The names in the book have been changed, but the situations are real. I want to give you a sense of what Attention Deficit Disorder feels and looks like, what it's like to have it, and what it's like to be around it. And, perhaps most important, I want to offer some very practical suggestions for what you can do about it.

◂ ◂ ◂ 1 ▸ ▸ ▸

Life with ADD: Personal Stories

▼

Jeremy's Story

▼

I remember my desk when I was a child. It was usually piled high with papers, toys—whatever I was working on. Once or twice a year my mother would make me clean it up, and it would feel so wonderful. Somehow I could have a new, fresh start. The fresh start would last maybe a day or two. Then I would start piling my homework on top of my desk and I'd think, oh no, here we go again. The homework would stop as soon as the desk was cluttered again. I had no idea what to do with the clutter. It seemed the best place to put it was on top of the desk.

Today, my office at home looks like my desk when I was a kid. I feel like it should be labeled a danger zone. It's so cluttered that when my son comes in, he trips on things. My wife, who's the complete opposite of me, doesn't want to look at it. She's embarrassed for people to see it. The fact that I've lived in that kind of environment for *ten years* seems ridiculous.

I feel ashamed. I'm frustrated as hell. I feel like I'm not a grownup yet. On days I have to do paperwork, I make myself sit at my desk and try to get organized. My desk is piled high. I pick up a bill, make it out, and start to put a stamp on it. But the stamps are next to the paper clip box and I think it should go in the desk, so I put it in the desk. And I see more pencils than I need, so I throw two of them out. Then the phone rings, and while I'm on the phone I start throwing out junk mail, and there are magazines on the desk, so I take them to the bookcase. In the bookcase there's an old magazine I don't need anymore so I throw that away. Then I realize that the waste basket is full so I empty it. When I go outside to empty the waste basket, I see that there's something going on in the kitchen, so I do something in there. It's like I'm following a trail from one thing to another.

I can't get anything done because I can't concentrate on any one task. I can't seem to determine that, ok, this is the time to get the file cabinet straightened out. My motivation is always crisis. What gets done is what has to get done. The invoices I have to send out to get paid get sent out. The bills I have to pay so the insurance company and the light company don't shut off services get paid. I'm always late for appointments. Bills get paid at the last moment, usually, like reports in school were done at the last minute. I pushed the limits then, and I still push the limits. But if I had my druthers, I wouldn't push the limits. I'd rather not file two extensions every year on my income tax.

But I seem to have no choice. I have a real lack of attention for things I'm not interested in. I have poor task completion and no organization. I seek immediate gratification with no long term goals. I've got no goal setting at all, really; I can't even set them. I just kind of fell into photography; I never sat down and said, ok, I want to be a photographer.

My file cabinet symbolizes my inadequacy for me. Ten years ago I was going to straighten it out. Now, ten years later, the file cabinet still isn't straightened out. Knowing that I can't organize my file cabinet—telling myself that I'm going to do it and knowing that I can't—drives me nuts. It makes me feel like I don't have any control over my life. It makes me feel ashamed and inadequate. It makes me feel frustrated and helpless. How big a deal is it to organize a file cabinet? We're not talking about brain surgery.

From society's point of view, I have the potential to accomplish so much more with my life, and I've come to see myself as lazy because I can't do certain tasks. Now I let my wife make the major decisions in my life—whether to buy a house, whether to have kids, how many to have. I just feel like I have no control over my life. Most of the time it doesn't bother me. But sometimes I get angry, really angry, and it comes out uncontrollably at my wife and my professional associates in sarcasm and shouting. I wish I knew what to do.

Jeremy Southland

12

Ann's Story

▼

I grew up not feeling very good about myself. In school, it was hard for me to stay on the subject or to finish anything. When I didn't finish my school work, I'd get spankings at home. Teachers would be on my back. They said I was such a good child—they couldn't understand it. And I tried so hard. I just couldn't finish anything. I couldn't concentrate. I couldn't take notes even if I really tried. I was distracted very easily by practically everything. If someone sneezed, I'd look at him and my mind would go off in a million directions. I'd look out the window, wondering why he had sneezed.

And my coordination wasn't good. When I was in the third grade, I got up to get a vase of flowers. I fell and spilled the water. I remember one time in art class we had to draw something. I really tried, but the teacher used mine as an example and said, "Look how bad hers is. She just goofed off." They used to hit me on the hands with a paddle because my handwriting was bad because I wrote so fast, even though I tried to slow down and write well. I was always walking fast and doing everything fast—just making a mess. There were so many things I couldn't do. People would say, "If you'd just try," but I was worn out from trying. It made me irritable. I felt like a failure.

The situation has persisted into adulthood. I'm very disorganized. Take housekeeping, for example. After dinner, when I start the dishes, I'll wash a little, then run and wipe off the table, wipe the cabinet, talk on the phone, and never get anything completed. I have to really concentrate and tell myself "You are going to get the dishes done." Then they get done, but I still get the urge to stop and go wash off the dining room table. Just like someone is pulling me. My closet and drawers are still a mess, just like when I was a kid.

What's really hard is to stay with any kind of paper work—bills, for example. It's my husband's job to do the bills. If it

13

were mine, we'd probably be in jail. He said he was going to do it because I made such a mess out of it. When I apply for a job, it's really hard for me to fill out the application. It's hard for my mind to stay focused. Only recently at age forty-five have I been able to sit down and write a letter. I usually write small postcards.

I'm the most impulsive person in the world. It gets me in trouble. If I see something I know I shouldn't buy, I'll buy it anyway. Or, I'll say something that I know the minute it comes out of my mouth I'm going to regret. I can't keep it from coming out. It's just got to come out. It's like a little monster. I'm bad about interrupting people. It seems like I have to get out what I'm going to say in a hurry.

I wish I could just slow down and relax. I have problems sitting still. I cannot just sit for two hours drinking coffee. During TV commercials I'm usually up fixing popcorn, getting something to drink, talking on the telephone, or wiping off the coffee table. People say I make them nervous, but I don't even realize I'm doing anything. That hurts my feelings. I don't want to be different.

My dream has always been to be some kind of counselor, but I felt like I wasn't college material, so I got married and had two children. I have a real estate license now. I don't know how I passed the test. I must have guessed right. What I like about selling is that I'm always on the move and I love people. I'm tuned into them. But I'm too sensitive to have a sense of humor. I think I have a thin skin. I get my feelings hurt easily. When that happens, I cry and go into my shell.

My mood swings from high to low. I either feel very good or very down. I feel up if the house looks good. If I get everything done that I think I should, it makes me feel good about myself. I feel responsible for a lot of people. If my husband is in a bad mood, or if things aren't going right for my kids, my mother, or my sister, I feel bad. I don't know what's wrong with me.

Ann Ridgley

Jack's Story

▼

I feel like I'm constantly building a house of cards, a very unstable structure. Other people can glue their cards together, but I can't. It's so hard to come to a firm decision because I don't trust myself to tell what is right, what is acceptable. And when I do reach a decision, it's after hemming and hawing around.

There's never a moment's peace. I feel like I'm always juggling things. When I'm dealing with a customer in my business, for example, establishing a relationship. If that customer gets mad, even though I may know it has nothing to do with me, I'm crushed. I always try to avoid the action that makes him mad. Second guessing runs my whole life.

That's what I mean by a house of cards. Other people could just shrug off the anger. I can't. I blame myself, usually. Or I blame someone else. Blame's a big part of my life. Things go wrong a thousand times a day. If I don't blame other people, I have to blame myself. Because of it, I've never developed self-esteem. I'm always seeing what's wrong and always critical of myself.

And if I'm continually running through life, building these houses of cards and making sure they don't fall down, when somebody else knocks them down, I'm enraged. But I only express my anger at home, where it's safe because someone loves me there. I can explode over little things and they allow that because they understand me.

I can take just so much of the daily pressures of life; then I go numb, physically and emotionally. I don't know what it's like not to be mentally tired. Life wears me out. I need to get away from it, and alcohol is a way. Sometimes I just need to get drunk. Sometimes I withdraw and fall into a depression. Other people don't understand, and because they don't, they

15

think it's ridiculous. What dummy in his right mind is going to go through life doing this to himself?

It hurts so bad. How many times can I hit myself with a hammer? Other people seem able to just sluff off things they don't want to feel. I can't. Everything's important. Internally, I have no stability. I don't know who is right and who is wrong. Once I make a decision, I feel like my back is to a wall. When my decision gets altered, I can't accept it. That's why I grew up with my parents saying "I can't tell you anything. You're so stubborn, you won't give an inch. Everything has got to be your way. You're self-centered." I don't know what I'm going to do.

Jack Cooper

Lisa's Story

▼

In the fourth grade there was a girl named Karla. She was so sweet. She could be quiet and she could sit still, and all her teachers loved her. She never even had to try to get people to like her.

My dream was to be like Karla. But I never even made it into the classroom. I was always acting up, getting into a fight with someone, not paying attention, and doing things that would take me off the task. I just wanted to be heard. At home I was the one everyone pointed at and said, "You're weird." I'd want to be just like everyone else, but someone would point out something about me they thought was weird, and I'd get upset.

It's still that way. I'm still learning how to shut out things that distract me. It's hard for me to stay on task. When I started as a DJ, I worked at a local station. There was so much going on that there was always something to keep my attention. I could keep focused on the tasks. But when I got promoted, I had technical assistants to do most of the tasks. It was then that I ran into trouble. I had less to do that held my attention so I found myself drifting off during the songs, since they were all I had to concentrate on.

Next, I got my own talk show. It was great being on the air because there was lots to do that would hold my attention. But preparing for the show was something else. I'd get distracted at home going through all the latest local and national newspapers because I couldn't concentrate on one story at a time.

It was a long time before I started booking guests in advance. I was always waiting until the last minute. I put it off because there were decisions to make. What if I made the wrong one? I have a lot of expectations—perfectionism—and I wanted things to be a certain way. What if I chose the wrong one? A part of me said, "I just won't make any decisions at all." I'm great at making schedules, but it's hard for me to stay on one.

I'm one of those people who are all of a sudden switching topics in a conversation. It leads to some bizarre conversations. I really treasure friends who can keep up with me. Some people just look at me like I'm crazy.

I feel like I'll never be at the same level everybody else is on. I'm always behind, in the sense that they can get on a path and travel that path and get to the end. Me, I'll go to the right, then to the left, and then I'll get back on the path. Eventually I'll get to the end, but I never travel a straight line. I feel that if I could travel a straight path, I would be farther ahead than I am. And I beat myself up because of it.

My world was too painful, so I got into a lot of stuff that I shouldn't have—to tone down the pain. I'm better now, but emotionally I still have to work with the pain. If someone says, "You're so outrageous," it may be a compliment, but I perceive it as "You're so weird," just like when I was a kid. That hurts. I have to ask what they mean. Is it good or bad? I still get angry, but not as angry as I used to. I don't try to be Karla anymore.

Lisa Connell

◂◖◀ 2 ▶◗▸

The Hidden Disorder

▼

*F*orty-two-year-old Jason had come to see me for treatment of chronic depression. After a half dozen visits, I could see that my usual ways of doing therapy weren't working as expected. He was placed on antidepressant medication for persistent depression after a psychiatric consultation, but he remained the ineffectual Jason I'd come to know. Most people would have shown an improvement by then, or I at least would have identified the cause of the distress.

But Jason had me stumped. I was becoming increasingly tense around him, and not just out of wounded professional pride. Physically, there was nothing smooth about Jason. He was restless during our meetings. He continually jiggled his foot and shifted his weight in his chair. His eyes darted around the room. His mind jumped, with no continuity, from one topic to another.

Though he was bright, educated, and seemingly well-socialized, Jason's self-esteem was extremely low. He felt, and I agreed, that he had not lived up to his potential. He was unable to organize his life. He shifted from one uncompleted business to another, and, in fact, demonstrated an inability to stick with any project or subject for long. His wife reported that he lacked follow-through even at intimate times.

Jason complained that he kept getting distracted from his personal goals by whatever was happening in his immediate environment. He couldn't screen out the things that didn't matter. On the way to write checks for his bills, he would be drawn to the window by a tweeting bird, and then he would notice the overgrown grass in the backyard, which required a trip to the gas station to get gas for the lawnmower, which would lead to a conversation with the station owner about his wife's operation, which turned the short trip into an afternoon expedition, leaving him little time to either pay the bills, as he originally (and with good intentions) had set out to do, or to mow the lawn.

The world was a booming, buzzing, confusing place to Jason, and his relief was to run, literally. He had become a marathon runner, practicing almost daily, running until he was exhausted. Then, in this burnt-out state, he'd stop his fidgeting and fall asleep in front of the TV or within moments of going to bed.

Exploring his family history, I learned that Jason's parents had bailed him out of scrape after scrape, all caused by his seemingly irresponsible, undisciplined behavior. But he paid a high price for their assistance. He was always viewed as "poor Jason" and "the black sheep." These were labels he couldn't escape. His wife had simply picked up where his parents had left off.

His mess of a life wasn't something that Jason felt he could do much about. No matter how hard he tried, he kept messing up. He had come to believe he was just a bad person.

He was wrong. As I watched him sit in his chair fidgeting, observed his short attention span and easy distractibility, and learned of his childhood disasters and compulsive need to run, I began to get a glimmer of what was going on. Finally, though it went against my professional training and everything I'd been taught, I tentatively diagnosed Jason as an adult suffering from untreated Attention Deficit Disorder.

◀ What Is ADD?

Attention Deficit Disorder is a debilitating, little-recognized, and widespread condition that is surrounded by confusion and debate in the professional community. For decades, clinicians have believed that ADD disappears entirely with the onset of puberty. Others believed it declines in prevalence, disappearing in about half the cases. Now, a growing body of research indicates that it is a lifelong condition, a belief which I hold strongly. I've watched my own son reach late adolescence with his ADD intact.

Like Jason, the adult with ADD is a mass of unfinished tasks, broken promises, and unfulfilled potential, subject to uncontrollable temper outbursts, fidgeting, resistance to being touched, and a tendency toward drug and alcohol abuse or other compulsive behavior. His behavior both creates and expresses a deep frustration and confusion, and a fearful sense of not being in control of his life.

My adult patients with ADD complain of an inability to cope with the stresses of life. They complain of chronic and unspecified emotional pain, and, like Jason, they may experience deep depression over their unfulfilled potential. Their frustration and uncontrolled temper may show up as child or spouse abuse or be expressed in other criminal acts. Friendships and family relationships are rocky and often fail.

An official definition of ADD-RT (Residual Type, which applies to adults) can be found in *Psychiatric Annals* 16: January, 1986, pp. 23–28, in an article by David Woods, M.D., entitled "The Diagnosis and Treatment of Attention Deficit Disorder Residual Type." It states that an adult *first must have exhibited ADD symptoms as a child.* After that the person must:

1) Have attention span deficiency.

2) Have motor abnormalities.

3) Have at least two of the following symptoms:
    poor impulse control, low stress tolerance
    with emotional over-reaction to the stress,
    poor organization with poor task completion,
    extreme mood swings in response to events in
    the external environment, or short, excessive
    temper.

From time to time, we all experience at least a mild form of each of these symptoms as we go through life. Occasionally we are distracted from the task at hand. In business meetings we may fidget a little as we long to get on with other projects that carry pressing deadlines. And none of us are strangers to bad moods, occasional impulsive gestures, or taking on a task without being well organized.

But, for the person with ADD, it's not a matter of occasionally. It's a way of life.

Sometimes persons with ADD are able to constructively manage their behavior. They learn to work around it, and, in a few cases, to use it to their advantage, such as the high-powered, on-the-go salesperson or entrepreneur, or the comic who entertains nonstop.

More often, however, by adolescence many people with ADD have found drugs, alcohol, or other means to self-medicate or mask the symptoms of ADD, which often reappear after the removal of the masking substance or activity.

Even worse, many ADD adults, like Jason, are very strongly socialized to do "right," so much so that they begin to inhibit their behavior over all so that they won't draw criticism. They learn to hide their ADD. But, as with Jason, in the process they also hide much of their potential and become chronically depressed.

The symptoms exhibited during childhood don't disappear. They simply take on a different guise.

Controlling temper is one of the areas in which adults with ADD often learn to mask their problem. They may "control" their tempers in the setting that causes their anger, but display them later, at home for example. Consequently, seemingly small things can really set them off, and others wonder how they can be so irritable or angry. Yet their anger disappears as quickly as it appears; it is unlikely to persist day after day or week after week.

We know that all hyperactive children also have ADD (but not all children with ADD are hyperactive). While the hyperactivity may diminish, the motor abnormality that accompanies ADD does not. But as the person matures, this motor abnormality may be more subdued, or it may be channelled differently. Like Jason, the adult with ADD may fidget almost constantly, tapping a finger, swinging a foot, or shifting his or her weight in a chair. Adults with ADD typically are a restless lot, always on the go, and they may not be able to relax unless they are dead tired. They're either going full-blast or they're nearly comatose. If they're not on the move, they may fall asleep almost immediately.

Adults with ADD most typically have poor attention when doing tasks not inherently interesting to them. But with activities they find interesting and enjoyable, their attention may be normal. This may sound like a failing in self-discipline, but it's not. Remember, they can be distracted easily by whatever is going on around them. Young adults, for example are often quite good at video games, but terrible at higher mathematics, such as algebra, which requires multiple steps to reach a solution. Many ADD adults have difficulty sustaining a conversation with others, particularly in groups. Listening to verbal reports and lectures becomes overtaxing, and so they give up trying. Poor attention span can severely limit their intellectual and vocational achievements.

Poor impulse control in adults may express itself in their spending or drinking habits. They may be so-called impulse-buyers, often with dire financial consequences, and their impulsive approach to drinking can lead to chemical abuse. The "spur of the moment" is their constant goad. They may speak out of turn in conversation, seeming to interrupt without considering the feelings of others.

◄ How Many Americans Suffer From ADD?

Professional estimates vary significantly, from 2% to 22% of the total population. In consulting with dozens of colleagues, I've heard estimates that cluster closer to the top number.

The number of adults with ADD may be far greater than generally suspected (and I believe it is), but the truth is, we don't know how many Americans suffer from ADD. There are several reasons for this.

It wasn't until the late 1970s that the possibility was raised that ADD continued into adulthood. Until then, most clinicians believed that it simply disappeared with the onset of puberty. Recent studies indicate that fully 80% of children diagnosed as having ADD warrant a similar diagnosis in early adulthood. Other studies estimate that 50% to 70% of children diagnosed with ADD between six and twelve years of age continue to show symptoms through middle adolescence; the prevalence declines to about 35% in late adolescence and further diminishes through adulthood.

Such studies are steps in the right direction, but they don't capture the full truth, from my point of view. I believe ADD is a lifelong condition. You don't outgrow it. It never disappears. My own son has reached late adolescence with his ADD intact. His father, a practicing psychologist in his fifties, has reached maturity with his ADD intact. So have hundreds of other adults whom I've treated or diagnosed. (Jason was my first ADD adult diagnosis, not my last.)

Another factor in our inability to get a better estimate is the lack of a "data bank" on ADD. The literature is spotty, scattered, and notably lacking in numbers. We don't know how many children or adults are diagnosed with ADD.

ADD is difficult to diagnose. Some professionals term it a convenient misnomer for a whole list of symptoms that can be attributed to a cluster of disorders. We also don't know how often it has been misdiagnosed, because of our misunderstanding of its continuity into adulthood. We don't know how many people should be diagnosed with it. Much of the ADD in children is not caught. Teachers aren't trained to spot it. Neither are truant officers or parents. Rather, the outward display of the disorder is dismissed as errant behavior or immaturity. Among adults, it has often been misdiagnosed as any of several other disorders that share some of the symptoms.

◀ What Causes ADD?

No one knows yet. Research thus far demonstrates that there is not one simple causative factor or trigger. Rather, genetic influences tend to be interrelated with environmental factors such as heavy metal (especially lead) toxicity. The 1980s provided research data that suggest some genetically transmitted neurochemical abnormalities in the brain. Though author Dr. Alan Zametkin hesitates to use the word "cause," a study by scientists at the National Institute of Mental Health indicates that a specific brain abnormality has been found in people with hyperactivity. Their brains seem to be less active, especially in areas controlling concentration and impulsive behavior. The results were seen as an advance but not the final word.

Clinical Psychiatry News (August 1987) reported that a computerized EEG distinguishes between Attention Deficit Disorder and depression, "providing compelling evidence that psychological dysfunction alone cannot explain many patients' conditions and that biological evaluation is necessary. . . . Something is physiologically wrong."

First and second generation offspring are seen to be affected by the results of hormonal, infectious, or other compromises to individual parents or grandparents. Genetically transmitted neurobiochemical abnormalities are purported to be at the root of behavioral disorders such as ADD, though interaction of genetic and environmental factors must be taken into account.

Attention deficits most likely represent signs of disorganized central nervous system function and are invariably affected (exacerbated or ameliorated) by environmental and social factors. Obviously what causes ADD is not a simple matter. For more information, consult the following sources, on which I have relied for this section:

Bonnet, Kenneth A., Ph.D. "Learning Disabilities: A Neurobiological Perspective in Humans, " *Pro-Ed Journal*, 1989.

Coleman, William L., M.D., and Levine, Melvin D., M.D., "Attention Deficits in Adolescence: Description, Evaluation and Management," *Pediatrics In Review*. Vol. 9 no. 9, March 1988, p. 287.

Hussey, Hans R., M.D., "A Different Perspective on the Epidemiology of Psychiatric Disorder." Department of Psychiatry, University of Vermont College of Medicine, Burlington, Vermont.

Painter, Kim. "Brain Flaw Key to Hyper Children," *New Journal of Medicine*, November 15, 1990.

Clinical Psychiatry News, Vol. 15, No. 8, August, 1987.

◀ Who Has ADD?

Because ADD may be genetically transmitted, it is important that family history be gathered for an accurate diagnosis: parents may pass ADD on to their children. Sometimes it may skip a generation, or even two, before showing up again. It strikes all classes and groups.

The abnormal chromosome structure has been thought to occur from four to twelve times more often in males than in females. Though I tend to agree, based on my own observations, that it is more prevalent in men, the assertion is open to question. Possibly, the behavioral characteristics are not as easily observed in women, are not as classic, or may be diagnosed as histrionic or unstable behavior.

◀ Why Be Concerned About ADD?

For each person directly affected by ADD, there are millions more—family and friends, employers and citizens—who suffer financially and emotionally because of the condition.

The high stress that untreated ADD creates often leads to addictions, or excesses, in all forms including eating, spending, and working, that compromise the person's physical and mental health. After recovering from chemical abuse involving drugs or alcohol, abusers often demonstrate underlying ADD symptoms. And the impulsive tendency of people with ADD raises the odds of illegal and thoughtless behavior, which costs the taxpayer.

ADD interferes with the educational process. Those afflicted generally, but by no means always, perform poorly in school and contribute greatly to the dropout rate, although they tend to be intelligent.

In my practice I see the ones who *are* bright. The others may have already dropped out of school and can't afford treatment. It would be interesting to make a study of prison populations to determine the incidence of ADD.

For the employer, lost work days, increased insurance rates, and low morale are other consequences. Adults with ADD often change jobs frequently. One ADD adult I treated had twelve jobs in eight years. This contributes to the high cost of unemployment insurance and to the high cost of doing business.

The family of an untreated ADD person suffers most, perhaps. Marital conflict, seemingly constant disruption in the household, and spouse or child abuse are all fall-out from trying to maintain relationships with an adult with untreated ADD. The human heartache is enormous.

◂ı◀ı◀ 3 ▶ı▶ı▸

The Abuse

▼

*A*s a result of the disorder's obscurity, people with ADD are often scape-goats; misunderstood and mistreated. They go through life hearing comments like:

"She doesn't finish what she starts."

"He's irresponsible."

"She's smart, but just doesn't settle down."

"He never follows through."

"She won't let me comfort her when she's upset."

"He falls asleep watching TV the moment he comes home."

"She doesn't realize I'm tired, too."

"He's so immature."

The inference of this kind of comment is that the ADD person can "do it" if he just tries. Not so, or, at least, not without adjustment because of his ADD.

◀ What Causes This Abuse

Words like lazy, moody, unmotivated, irresponsible, too sensitive, clumsy, troublesome, insecure, and temperamental are common in descriptions of adults with undiagnosed ADD. Rarely are such characteristics recognized as only the result of neurochemistry that has never allowed the person satisfactory achievement or the luxury of living up to his potential. More commonly, the visible signs of ADD are seen as flaws in the behavior or even the moral fiber of the person.

◄ What Is Abuse?

To be abused means to be treated badly or unfairly, and, largely through misunderstanding, it happens to people with ADD physically, psychologically, and verbally.

Physical abuse (unless wretchedly out of control) is most easily understood by the victim and is the easiest to work with therapeutically. Psychological abuse puts the individual down and questions his self worth and value, and is perniciously invasive. It convinces the person the abuse is deserved because of intrinsic wrongness within him. Psychological abuse is often experienced as the most confusing form of abuse because of its subtle nature; therefore, evidence of it is hardest to identify in the adult initially. Once identified, however, it can be dealt with, and early beliefs can be reprogrammed. Verbal abuse—name calling such as "dumb" or "clumsy"—gives the person a false identity. The individual soon comes to believe the labels to be accurate descriptions. Then they tend to live up to these labels. This is called the self-fulfilling prophecy. Psychotherapy can eradicate the sting of the hurtful words and replace them with supportive ones.

To understand how the abuse takes place and what forms it takes, let's start with the ADD person's experience from birth.

◄ Abuse of the Child

The abuse often begins when the person with ADD is a baby, and it comes in a subtle form: rejection. Because of their extreme sensitivity to touch and other external stimuli, the stroking, patting and jiggling that comforts many babies doesn't work very well with many ADD infants. Rocking the baby to sleep, usually a wonderful experience for parent and baby alike, may stimulate an ADD baby to waken. Parents can become just as edgy about being rejected as babies can, and so they may withdraw from their newborns when their overtures are rebuffed.

The abuse, again unintentional, may intensify as the child grows. It generally happens for two quite different reasons: The oversensitivity of the child means that he feels parents' and society's interventions more keenly than other children. Then, the child with ADD, laboring under poor impulse control and overreactivity, creates more situations that bring adult attention and negative reinforcement.

Take Marcus, for example. At age nine, his life had been rapidly disintegrating, and, not yet diagnosed as having ADD, he did not know why. He only knew that his inability to concentrate was bringing daily scoldings in the classroom, which were systematically eroding his self-esteem. He was also on the basketball team. Because of his general behavior, mostly prompted by the ADD, he was also losing esteem in the eyes of his teammates, and began to suffer that painful harassment that nine-year-olds are so good at handing out.

A well-socialized child, Marcus maintained control in the classroom, but by the time basketball practice rolled around, his control was just used up. One day, words mumbled under the breath of a fellow player, just loud enough for Marcus to hear, hit their mark. In a brief, uncontrolled moment, Marcus hurled his body at the boy who, unfortunately, tripped over his own growing feet, fell back, and bumped his head on a brick wall.

No doubt frightened by the obvious show of violence, the coach gave no thought to how it started, and Marcus got it—a loud, embarrassing scolding. And Marcus retaliated with rich words questioning the coach's ancestry.

Marcus was already frightened by the result of his own reactions. He had only meant to shove the kid to get him to shut up, not push his head into the wall. Then he felt further assaulted by the coach's words, trapped by misunderstanding—and alone. He did the only thing he knew how to do. He walked away. But even this he was later criticized for, because he did not "take his medicine."

Since Marcus could not control his behavior, the child felt quite victimized by the adult's negative attention. The incident left the marks of abuse.

Parents, with the best intentions, just as unthinkingly play their role in the abuse of their growing ADD child. It's natural for us to want to be proud of our children, and equally natural to communicate that desire to them. We expect them to produce in school so we can feel acceptable, and we expect the ADD child to achieve by being taught in the same way as non-ADD children—in a classroom with twenty-five other children. But what about the child who cannot screen out external stimuli? He's still told it's his responsibility to pay attention. When he doesn't, because he can't, the abuse may come in the form of well-meant scoldings or behavioral limits that the child can't abide—groundings or being kept after school. Of course, at times the abuse may be much more severe than that, from overreactive responses (remember, many children with ADD may have an undiagnosed parent who is also volatile, susceptible to frustration, and overreactive) such as groundings for weeks on end, to actual physical punishment.

Such abuse may rise from completely benign circumstances, but it's abuse nonetheless, and a legacy of scoldings and blame from teachers and parents remains for life. I don't mean to blame the teachers or parents. Their purpose is good and decent, namely, to properly raise the child. But they become frustrated, and reasonably so at times, at their failure to do so.

◀ The Legacy of Abuse

How does such childhood abuse show up in adults? Often, it takes the form of self-abuse, including low self-esteem, under achievement, and addictive behavior. Take Jennifer, who has been in an entry level, civil service position for five years despite having a college degree. She has low self-esteem and doesn't believe she's capable of doing any better. She was often told she was "dumb" and would only be able to do the simplest of jobs. This verbal abuse stunted her self-confidence. Or take George, a successful salesman who starts drinking every day at noon. As a child, he'd been labeled lazy and repeatedly punished at home and at school for not finishing his school work. Without alcohol, he felt the pain of the switchings and rapped knuckles and the anxiety of childhood every time he entered a place of business. George had been physically and emotionally abused.

◀ ADD and Procrastination

At times it seems that everyone—spouse, family, and employer—is angry with the adult with ADD, and all for the same reason: procrastination. It can be perceived as thoughtlessness or laziness, but it is still procrastination. The wife or husband feels that personal needs aren't being met. The employer doesn't understand why projects are incomplete, why deadlines are not met. The criticism isn't long in coming.

Procrastination, in reality, is many things, none of which is lazy or, necessarily, thoughtless. In therapy circles, procrastination is traditionally considered to be a learned fear response. It may be a response to trying to do what you should when you really don't want to do it (also called resistance). It may be rebellion against an authority figure. Sometimes it is a fear of failure, fear that work turned in will not be acceptable.

Such reasons are indeed sometimes valid explanations for ADD persons who put off work. Remember, they are more susceptible to the fear of failure than the general population, because they've often had more experience with failure. But, with the ADD profile in mind, consider another reason why they "appear" to procrastinate: Distractibility. They begin a project with good intentions and plenty of time, but they get distracted before they complete it. This only leads to more criticism from others, so that criticism and abuse haunt the person with undiagnosed ADD from infancy through child-hood and on into adulthood.

◂ ◀ ◀ **4** ▶ ▶ ▸

The Inner Pain

▼

*P*ersons with ADD often are excruciatingly aware of their inadequacies (though they can't identify their source).

They know, perhaps better than anyone, the discrepancy between their potential and the actual level of their performance. This knowledge is a source of intense pain. Like people in the cases we've seen so far, they understood how to do a classroom task but simply couldn't concentrate long enough to get the job done. Usually, though, they were blamed for being wrong. Talk about helpless, gut-wrenching pain.

Later in life, as an adult, a person with ADD may have an idea that will solve his company's cash shortfall, but somehow he keeps getting distracted from mobilizing the information into a report for his boss. Talk about frustration. You can feel it in the pit of your stomach. And it's doubly painful because he remembers the feeling from his childhood.

◀ Grief

The inability to live up to potential creates a sense of loss. And, like all losses in our lives, the loss of ability means we're in for the emotions of grief.

With grief, we normally go through several stages of emotion—denial, anger, bargaining, depression—that end with a healthy resolution—acceptance of our loss. After that, we go on to live full and happy lives. Often we need—and receive—assistance in working through our grief.

But in undiagnosed and untreated ADD persons, the grief has seldom been worked with because the loss hasn't been recognized. As a consequence, they may get caught up in the anger or depression that are a natural part of the loss and grief cycle. Originally, for people with ADD, the unresolved anger and depression may be felt only in relation to school work. Then they are likely to generalize to any learning situation or expected task. Finally, they may generalize even further, until they are angry or depressed all the time.

◀ Anger

Very often the emotion we see in persons with ADD is anger: Explosive tempers set off by seemingly small incidents—or no incident at all, at least in the eyes of others.

Persons with ADD suffer from anger for a variety of reasons, certainly, and unresolved grief is one of them. Another reason is that ADD makes a person less effective than he or she otherwise would be, which leads to frustration. And because ADD is beyond the control of the individual, there is a sense that life is out of control, which causes feelings of helplessness. Both frustration and helplessness hurt—a lot. And anger comes automatically as a defense against the hurt. But there's always some other feeling under the anger—helplessness, hopelessness, fear, or frustration.

◀ Flooding

There's another factor behind the anger we see in unresolved ADD—the emotional flooding persons with ADD experience.

The phrase "thin-skinned" was tailor-made for the ADD person. His emotional skin is paper-thin and does not block stimuli that come at him, nor does it deflect incoming particles of experience. Instead, his porous system absorbs instantly all that is in the environment, and the absorption is so fast and intense and pervasive that it "floods" the person.

The sensation of flooding threatens and confuses the person with ADD and he reacts—almost in desperation, as if to save his life, for that is how it feels to him.

He is aware of everything that's going on around him and "wears his feelings on his sleeve." Though often labeled over-reactive, the ADD person really isn't, when we factor in his thin skin. He overreacts only by common standards, but considering the intensity of the feelings he experiences, his reactions make sense.

This vulnerability to hurt leaves the person with ADD in need of protection which often takes the form of temper outbursts and striking out over the slightest thing. "Push away the hurt" says the outburst. Often, the cause of the outburst is overlooked, but it's always there. A defense? You bet, and much needed until the person can develop other, more effective defenses with fewer side effects.

◀ Confusion

In a person with untreated ADD, you are likely to find the sadness of being blamed for not paying attention, the hurt of being scolded, put down, or even physically punished for work not done—because the work could not be done. You may find the helplessness of not understanding what went wrong or what could have been done to change it. You may find, too, an utter hopelessness.

Often, however, you find confusion. "Why is she angry with me?" asks the husband. "I was doing the best I could." As in the case of the man who sets out to pay the bills and take his wife to dinner, but who ends up in conversation at the gas station while she's wondering where he is, the feeling is confusion. Why are you angry with me? Why can't I just concentrate on what I'm supposed to think about? Why can't I go from point A to point B without a lot of distractions? Why is my life such a mess?

Remember, people with undiagnosed and untreated ADD find the world a booming, buzzing place. They are unable to discipline their environment—to screen out the unwanted stimuli that invade their lives. And it's not just the world that confuses them. It's their response to it.

◀ Low Self-esteem

Maybe the single most common characteristic among people with ADD is low self-esteem. With a past of endless failure, projects started and never finished, and being constantly at odds with their parents, siblings, teachers, and bosses, they tend to think of themselves as bad characters, deficient, aimless, lazy—embracing the terms and characterizations others use to describe them.

◀ Rigidity

Right or wrong, ADD sufferers seem inflexible, seem to lack finesse, and will pursue a course of action without regard to the consequences. Their sensitivity and anger can be like blinders, with their impulsiveness acting like a goad to drive them down a path to self-destruction. To them, it may be the rational, moral action to take, but to us it appears reckless.

Consider the case of Lenny, just diagnosed with ADD and beginning therapy:

Lenny is 23, a college graduate, a bit of a hot-head, and turning into a very good salesman. He likes selling and liked his job until recently, when his old boss was transferred and a new one moved in.

The old boss was a kind, compassionate man who trusted Lenny, and if he had something to say to Lenny, he never sounded like he was criticizing him. And he extended generosity to other sales people. Sales reports were normally due by two o'clock Friday, but the boss extended the deadline for one salesman, who always had lunch with his daughter on Friday. The salesman was divorced and missed his daughter very much, and lunching with her was important to him. Extending the report deadline for him was no problem for anyone.

When the new boss came on board, it was another story. The man was a critical, toe-the-line kind of guy who raised his voice whether he needed to or not and felt obligated to point out that he was boss. Even before he got to know anyone, he started handing out orders. Reports—all reports—had to be in by two o'clock Friday. When the salesman who had lunch with his daughter politely asked for an extension of one hour, explaining the circumstances, the new boss gruffly replied "No extensions, no exceptions. A job is a job and if you can't do it, I'll find someone who can."

All the other sales people in the office glanced at each other but stayed quiet, burying their heads in their work. But Lenny, who already felt annoyed by the sound of the man's voice and attitude, couldn't stand it. It wasn't fair to his friend. No one else cared if the salesman's report was in by two o'clock.

Lenny got up and walked over to the new boss and right in front of everyone said, with raised voice, "That's not right. You shouldn't have done that. He's a good worker and it doesn't hurt anyone to extend his deadline. You have no right to do it."

The boss yelled "Sit down!" and Lenny stalked out of the office yelling "You're crazy. You've got no right to come in here and treat people that way."

39

When a friend tried to talk to him later, he was still hot under the collar and refused to apologize or back off. In fact, he quit the next day when, upon returning to pick up his worksheet for the day, he ran into his boss, who demanded an apology and started to lecture him. Lenny exploded and walked out, trapped by his ADD.

◀ Another Brand of Pain

I met Cynthia one evening at a middle-school parents' meeting. Disturbed and distracted by the chaotic approach to the session, my mind wandered over the day's events and my feet fidgeted. Cynthia, in contrast, looked so serene, unruffled by the politics of the organization and the lack of orderliness to the evening's agenda.

As I came to know Cynthia better, I came to understand that her quiet passivity was a cover for the wholesale confusion of ADD.

In reality, Cynthia was the over-controlled, passive type of ADD adult. She had crawled far inside herself, away from the world around her. It was the only way she could cope with the pain of ADD.

And, she had so restricted her environment that her ADD simply didn't show except when you got to know her intimately. All the symptoms were there. Her newsletters were always late, and, though she had a terrible struggle getting them together, she would accept no help. Not out of obstinacy or self-reliance, but out of shame. She didn't want anyone to see her work habits—which were like a page out of science fiction. Her home, too, was total chaos.

Cynthia's sense of competence was very low, which made her feel that she didn't quite belong. But she covered her discomfort by seeming a bit of a know-it-all at times, which put others off.

40

Her way of coping with ADD had shaped her personality, if not robbed her of it, for she had, in fact, sacrificed her personality at the altar of ADD.

Adults with ADD feel angry, frustrated, confused, and out of control. They can be chronically depressed—stuck in their grief, but grief over what they don't know. Their fear of failure—as Cynthia shows us—is enormous and repressive. And no wonder, when we consider how their lives have been filled with failure. Why *would* anyone so used to failure want to undertake new experiences or enter new situations that seem to set them up for yet more failure?

Where most of us feel moments of low self-esteem, the ADD person feels it all the time; it is a permanent state of being, and it causes him or her great pain.

Such is the living hell of the ADD person.

◂ı◂◄ 5 ▸ı▸ıı▸

Living with an ADD Person

▼

*H*aving ADD is terribly painful, but living with an ADD person presents a whole new set of problems. Consider this letter from the wife of a man with ADD:

Jack seemed like such a nice guy—agreeable, bright, well read, well educated and creative. His potential seemed enormous. He had big dreams and seemed to have all the skills needed to accomplish the task at hand—only he rarely did.

He worked a lot, don't get me wrong, but he somehow failed to get ahead as far as it seemed that he could or should. It frustrated him, and the more frustrated he became, the more he pulled into himself. He began to appear more of a taker than a giver—a bottomless pit. Rarely did he get it together enough to give back.

Resentment at his not giving back became my major emotion—and resentment on Jack's part grew as my expectations pressed him. He wasn't getting enough out of his own life to have anything left over for anyone else.

I know now, after the divorce, that he had ADD, and that he didn't have anything left to give. But I didn't know that then. Not that he was mean or anything like that. Jack didn't blow up. He just withdrew, spending large amounts of time

43

watching movies and television. Though he didn't exactly seem lazy (since he was willing enough to go out and earn a living) he seemed to have no time for household chores, self-care, or quiet conversation. In fact, he often fell asleep as soon as he sat down in the evenings.

His social skills seemed flawed. Some of that had to do with the give-and-take required of socializing, but there was something more. He didn't plan ahead, often acted impulsively, and seemed unable to orchestrate spontaneous enterprises so they would come off successfully.

I'll give you an example, one that happened after the divorce. Our son had an out-of-town football game and Jack offered to pick me up after work for the hour-long drive. The invitation came the afternoon of the game. I remembered the problems from the past, how he had trouble getting places on time. But I said "Fine," and added "It's very important to me to get there for the start of the game." Jack agreed.

The game began at 7:30 PM. I suggested we set out at 5:30 so there would be time to grab a bite to eat. He said "Okay." Then he arrived at six o'clock. But there was still plenty of time. As we headed down the freeway, he suddenly exited. "Where are you going?" I asked. "Home to change clothes," Jack said.

Again I said, "Jack, it's very important to me to get to the game on time."

"I know," he said.

Jack changed quickly enough so that we still had time to go to a fast-food place. But, leaving his apartment, he started to turn right at the corner rather than left to go back to the freeway. When I asked where he was going, he said "to get chicken" and named a restaurant several miles out of the way. I remembered how fussy Jack was about his food and how picking a place to eat could become a major stumbling block to peace. But getting to the game on time was a higher priority,

44

so I said, "That'll take too long. Let's go on. Maybe we'll find a chicken place in the town."

If my response seems like incredible forebearance, it wasn't. In the old days, I'd have been boiling with frustration, anxiety, and disappointment. But, by now, I realized that Jack wasn't trying to be difficult. Nor was he trying to be mean. He just seemed unable to be aware of my needs even though— through therapy—I'd learned to speak them clearly. Just like always, he was getting off the track he'd agreed to. I used to think it was because he agreed to things he didn't want. Or that he was being resistant to me on purpose. But, after I came to understand ADD, I realized it was neither. He just didn't get things done efficiently.

We arrived at the town sooner than expected and cruised around because he wanted to see what restaurants there were to choose from. I wanted to stop at the first place we found just so we could get to the game on time. But that wouldn't do for Jack. His feelings of being cheated, something that grew out of his ADD, often had spilled over into other areas, and he was fussy about buying anything. What made him a good shopper in other situations was maddening in this one.

Finally, we got back to the first place we'd seen and I nudged him into accepting it. Though we ordered our food to go, he, without thinking, ordered something that was complicated to get together. With kickoff time fast approaching, he leisurely added salad bar toppings to his food and, then, midstream, became distracted by the potato bar. As I watched, I realized he wasn't being mean. He just couldn't help it. But I remembered why I'd divorced him and reminded myself to drive my own car next time there was an out-of-town game. We were late to the game. Shades of an angry, frustrating past.

Those who live with an untreated, undiagnosed ADD person are very often victims of the condition as well. Whether the keynote to the ADD personality is flaring temper, unpredictability, chemical addiction, or constant disorganization, the behavior is extremely difficult to cope with, even for

45

caring and sensitive people. Unaware that the condition exists, parents, spouses, and siblings can become resentful and angry; they can feel exploited, disappointed, or cheated. None of these feelings make for healthy relationships.

◄ The Frustration

One teenager summed up how it was to live with his ADD brother: "It's frustrating."

Yes, that's a normal response to any sibling, but it's the ways in which the frustration comes out that makes the difference. I think the difference is in the "sharp corners" of an ADD personality. It's the abrasiveness that is so often present in relationships with an ADD person. It's their immediate "No" to most requests.

One brother mentioned how his ADD brother was prone to be combative. A mild pop on the arm became a "federal case" and was likely to be turned into a fight—maybe good-humored—but not one the ADD person could ever walk away from or be the first to stop. This included love pats that were interpreted as assaults instead of gestures of friendship.

Another sibling—a sister—talked about how her ADD sister tended to pick fights "out of thin air." Her view was representative of many others who noted in their siblings with ADD a tendency to make things happen when everything was quiet. Almost as if boredom threatened them, they seem to kick up dust for interest's sake.

◄ The Nuisance

The word "nuisance" also comes up frequently along with examples of attention-getting behavior. If five people are in a group, and one has ADD, that is the person who will unwittingly but most likely draw attention to himself.

Because they draw attention so easily, it's very easy for children to set up their brother or sister with ADD in the good guy/bad guy syndrome. Of course, any healthy sibling will jump at a chance to fight back in an argument, or at least gain brownie points with parents at the expense of the sibling. But when the sibling has ADD, it's not a fair contest.

◀ Don't Touch Me

Intimacy, so wonderful an experience for most of us, is often denied the people who live with an ADD person. For intimacy is a major challenge—if not an impossibility—for an ADD person.

They seem to feel everything excessively, from innuendos to touch. As babies, ADD persons are extremely sensitive. The normal things—rocking, holding, stroking—that a parent may do to soothe a baby don't work with an ADD baby. It upsets him. Thus, with no awareness of ADD, the parent may feel rejected by the baby, and intimacy is destroyed. Even as the child grows, his sensitivity to touch is unabated. Parents—and siblings—may be denied the familiarity of throwing a friendly arm around a shoulder.

And they may encounter a wall of distrust that goes beyond the physical. The person with ADD, battered by an unrelenting environment, may seek safety inside, withdrawing indiscriminately from friend and foe alike.

It's not just the ADD person's hypersensitivity that inhibits intimacy. Remember, they tend to be full on or full off. They can come home, plop down in front of the television, and be fast asleep in a couple of minutes. There is no chance for the development that leads to intimacy.

Sex with an ADD spouse can be something out of the one-minute manager's handbook. Frustrating? A nuisance? Destructive? You pick it.

47

◄ Who's to Blame?

The ADD person is almost obsessive about blame, for blame is the major perspective from which his life is structured. Some of this occurs, no doubt, from being chided for non-constructive behaviors in early life. Persons with ADD live with blame. They learn blame as a way of life. Also, it's simpler to take a frustrating experience and blame it on someone or something than to think through why and how things happen. Very likely the intensity of feeling experienced by the ADD person requires a short-circuited, quick resolution to the pain—and blame provides that.

But for those living with the ADD person, his need to blame is often experienced as hostile, needless—and painful—behavior. Most relationships are damaged by the placement of blame. It's no way to build trust, the glue of all relationships, and it sets a win-lose thinking in operation. You made me do it. I didn't do it. It wasn't my responsibility. It seems that the ADD person's finger is always pointed at those he lives with.

◄ The Damage

In practical terms, what all this boils down to for parents, spouses, siblings, and even friends is a wearing, tearing, thorn-in-the-side relationship.

Brothers and sisters see the ADD person's short attention span as a nuisance that gets in the way of peaceful, stable play activities. They see their ADD sibling getting in trouble a lot and often fall into the good kid/bad kid routine. The ADD children don't take orders well and tend to cause explosive situations. Their brothers and sisters who are non-ADD don't understand the disruption.

Mom and Dad tend to spend more time with their ADD child, though that time usually isn't constructive—so parents often get used to interacting with the child as a problem child. This can make parents feel guilty. I doubt there's a parent of an untreated ADD child who hasn't asked "Where did I go wrong?" What have I done?"

Face it: Living or working with a person with untreated, undiagnosed ADD is an angry, frustrating experience, full of disappointment, resentment, and dissatisfaction for all.

◂ ı ◂ı ◂ 6 ▸ı ▸ ı▸

The Quandary of Treatment

▼

*S*herry originally came into therapy wanting help with her second marriage. She was angry at her husband because he didn't take enough financial responsibility, and the children (his and hers) were erupting right and left. There were personal motivations, too. Her mood swings, evident all her life, seemed to be growing more extreme. Her ability to focus on a task and complete it seemed to have diminished rather than grown.

But she seemed eager to get things right in her life, ready to work at therapy. The only problem to the upbeat beginning was that Sherry had a different agenda every time she came in for therapy. Every time she agreed to work on an issue, something got in the way and follow-through was avoided. She would go off in a dozen directions the minute she walked out of my office.

Sherry's husband, though not as scattered, was no better than she was at follow-through. He made even bigger promises that he didn't keep. Working with the two of them was next to impossible.

Going through problems with each of their five children as the teenage years came on had left Sherry and her husband no

51

better able to take charge. They knew what to do, it seemed, but couldn't accomplish it.

Then the husband's financial irresponsibility left them in a lot of trouble which Sherry felt helpless to remedy. And Sherry, who for years had worked with her father (a drinker who had encouraged dependence in Sherry) was left without a job when he retired; the secure, if damaging, daily routine that had put structure in her life was eliminated.

Her husband's response was to face the music (his accountant and the IRS) and clean up his act. He stopped drinking, shaped up physically, and began to take responsibility in his business.

But it wasn't long after that that Sherry began drinking heavily and abusing her body in other ways—binging on caffeine products and eating and sleeping erratically. Other self-destructive behavior began to emerge. Sherry began to act out her feelings which meant, in her words, "pulling a runaway." She'd simply leave home, taking up with whomever she met. Maybe she'd have an affair; maybe just a friendship punctuated by emotional highs.

She'd claim great insights into her psychology from these episodes, but her scattered behavior didn't change, nor did her life smooth out. Much of the acting out was met with passivity by her husband, while her father supplied financial support so that Sherry could remain irresponsible. She continued being out of control for almost two years until she became an excessive financial liability and her mood swings (days spent in bed) had increased to the point where they could no longer be ignored. She was hospitalized four times during the next year.

Professionals who worked with Sherry disagreed about what was wrong with her. Their diagnoses ranged from alcoholism to Attention Deficit Disorder, manic-depression characterized by wide mood swings, and borderline personality characterized by a pervasive pattern of instability, with a few others thrown in for good measure.

Maybe they were all correct, for Sherry was a classic example of a person displaying multiple disorders, or at least the symptoms of such. Her childhood history—at school and in the family—indicated that she certainly had ADD. She was a member of a dysfunctional family riddled by addiction and codependency. Sherry never properly separated from her family of origin (parents) to become an independent person with value in her own right. She lived at a survival level most of the time, just barely able to show enough responsibility to get by. Her biochemistry was out of balance, in part because she did not attend to her nutrition, exercise, and rest, and, in part because there was something intrinsically wrong with her physically. Her mood swings, from extreme emotional highs to severe depression, were separated by periods of normal mood.

An extreme case? You bet, but Sherry's situation points up how difficult it can be to make a proper ADD diagnosis when other disorders may be present and symptoms may overlap. Organizational problems may be a sign of other learning disabilities. Mood variability can be the result of a biochemical imbalance having nothing to do with lifestyle. Impulsivity and overreactivity can be the result of a character disorder, such as borderline personality.

To further complicate the problem, mimicking symptoms may be present: Stress and emotional difficulties can mock many ADD symptoms such as inattentiveness, mood swings, low self-esteem, and anger.

Is it any wonder that a definitive diagnosis can be difficult? Sorting through the look-alike symptoms is confusing, and it's easy to reach for the closest and most general diagnosis available.

◀ What About Medication?

Even when an accurate diagnosis is made, treatment raises an argument among professionals.

Use of medication is common in ADD children, but, in ADD adults, its use is erratic, inconsistent, and, frankly, confusing even from the professional's point of view. Raise the question of medicating ADD adults in a group of mental health workers and you'll see the fur fly. I can't present a definitive statement on the use of medication, so my comments here are intended only to raise your consciousness about the issues.

I have heard contradictory statistical claims about the use of medication with adults, from "it never works" to "it works sixty percent of the time." Many ADD people initially have gained unexpected relief from their ADD symptoms when they used diet pills. They became, as one person put it, "instantly mature and responsible." Unfortunately, the relief lasts only as long as the supply of diet pills. Then they revert back to their old, familiar ADD behavior.

There is strong resistance to the use of the drug Ritalin. I have been told that, though commonly used in childhood ADD, it is *never* appropriate with adults. Yet I've seen a few people whose lives have been transformed because of its use. My own son did not reap the full benefits of nine months of counseling, which he received at age eleven, until he started taking Ritalin at thirteen. It helped him control his actions with less than gargantuan effort. Once on medication, he almost instantly showed the effects of counseling and could get himself to do what he really wanted to do all along. He never did want to be disruptive in groups or insensitive to the needs of others; he simply couldn't sit still. Once the medication allowed the therapy to take hold, however, he could show that he really was sensitive to others' needs.

I promise you, I have no vested interest in any particular drug being prescribed. But what does interest me is the strong reaction against it, unsubstantiated by research. As one physician put it, prescribing Ritalin "is just never done." Yet another practitioner I ran into was as extreme but in the opposite direction, diagnosing ADD willy-nilly in his patients—and treating them all with Ritalin.

Antidepressants, on the other hand, are often tried first as an adult ADD treatment—for those physicians who believe in the condition at all. In fact, several physicians I've run across not only preferred their use in treatment, but continued to prescribe their use whether they were effective or not on the patient's ADD (see the appendices, p. 181).

Another point of debate is drug treatment of ADD chemical abusers. Whether drug treatment can even be considered for this group is a legitimate question. Studies have shown a higher than normal incidence of addiction among people with ADD, but the reasons for this are unclear.

One thing's sure: Medication alone is inadequate to treat ADD. Counseling is imperative to teach the skills needed to manage ADD. There are no magic cures. ADD needs to be tackled every way possible.

◄ Therapy?

There is little precedent for the treatment of Attention Deficit Disorder in adults. Remember, clinicians have long been polarized on the question of whether ADD in adults (ADD-RT) is a reality. Many have been unwilling to look openly at the possibility that it exists. Indeed, beginning in the late 1970s, the bible of the American Psychiatric Association, the *Diagnostic Statistical Manual of Mental Disorders* designated ADD-RT as a viable diagnosis when Attention Deficit Disorder continued into adulthood. But when the DSM III-R came out in 1987, ADD-RT was eliminated. In its place was a listing of Undifferentiated ADD, with a note that research is necessary to determine if this is a valid diagnostic category and, if so, how it should be defined.

Just as challenging for the professional community has been arriving at a consensus on how to counsel ADD adults. First of all, there has been little therapy, counseling, teaching, or guidance of any kind available for ADD adults. Second, people

with ADD tend to be quite creative. Though they need structure, they also need to be involved in developing their own
structure so that they can carry it out independently. Thus,
traditional psychotherapy often doesn't work, and the results
of such attempts are often very uneven as the following case
indicates:

A woman who had been in treatment for almost two years
continued to cut deals with her husband, agreeing to be more
conscientious about running the house and managing the
affairs of everyday life. She and her therapist had determined that she really wanted these goals and intended to
follow through. They had examined unconscious motives
and childhood-connected reasons why she couldn't—or
didn't—follow through. They had looked at the marriage
with the concomitant issues of control and power and discovered that these issues were in balance. In short, they covered
every conventional base. Why, then, didn't the woman respond to the conventional therapy? You guessed it!

A bright business executive with a technical background repeatedly suffered emotional stress at work because he failed
to guide the people who worked under him through the com-
plex projects they were assigned. He could do the technical
part in his head but became overwhelmed and lost with the
myriad details that management requires. He would become
irritable and gripe at his people, and morale would plummet.
His home life, never smooth, suffered when "one more thing
requiring management" was necessary.

He was in individual psychotherapy as well as marriage counseling but continued to perform in dysfunctional ways. He
also became quite depressed as the counseling proved ineffective and was treated with antidepressants. They didn't do any
good, either.

There are other dangers in therapy. One therapist I know of
accurately diagnosed ADD in his clients but treated them in a
manner similar to that used with people in denial who suffer
from chemical abuse problems. He pressured his clients into

following a rigid structure he had developed. This approach, however, only kept clients coming to him for years because they remained dependent, helplessly trying to fit into his structure. Often their depression continued because they could not become independent of the therapist.

These are not uncommon instances; rather, they are common, and point out popular misconceptions and mistreatment in counseling persons with ADD, including:

◀ Regarding ADD as an emotional disorder rather than a physiologically based disorder that affects behavior.

◀ Misdiagnosis that results in treatment of childhood and parenting causes, behind which is the belief that ADD is the result of poor parenting or a dysfunctional family system.

◀ A belief that ADD people can control their behavior if they just want to. (This leads the therapist to focus on *why* people with ADD *don't want* to control their behavior.)

◀ Using insight therapy—training the ADD person in life skills rather than teaching the person how to recognize and accommodate the ADD.

◀ Failing to treat ADD after chemical abuse is stemmed.

◀ Marriage counseling that doesn't recognize the existence of ADD.

◀ Therapy that allows the therapist's own beliefs and prejudices about ADD to interfere with counseling.

Such is the quandary of ADD treatment.

◀ **Some Common Questions on the Treatment of ADD**

▶ **Will I become a zombie on medication?**

Absolutely not, if the kind and dosage is properly prescribed. Medications for Attention Deficit Disorder bring a person *up to par* so that his physical system can operate at a level closer to normal.

▶ **How can I find a therapist who can help me learn to live with my ADD?**

Unfortunately, that is not an easy task because very few psychotherapists or counselors have had training in working with adults who have ADD. Try locally first, checking with your Mental Health Association to see whether there is a support group established in your area. They will have a list of people who regularly treat the condition. If you have no luck, contact ADDendum newsletter, (914) 941-2661 or contact me, (214) 369-1104.

▶ **How can I find a doctor who could prescribe medication if it is indicated?**

Again, try through your local support group. Then ask your own physician for a referral that treats the condition. Ask your physician to become knowledgeable about ADD. Finally, reach out to one of the resources listed in this book.

▶ **Why does ADD show up so often after chemical abuse is treated? Does the chemical abuse cause ADD?**

No. If, indeed, ADD appears after a person has "dried out," it would have been there all along but simply wasn't visible. One of the reasons is that untreated people with ADD are prone to self medicate and one of the ways to do that is with alcohol or drugs. People with ADD are also prone to impulsive behavior and may more readily be swept along with the crowd, succumbing to peer pressure and thus establishing a chemical habit. (More research is necessary to determine whether there are biochemical connections between chemical addiction and ADD.)

It is important that an accurate diagnosis of ADD be made after chemical abuse has taken place because attention problems are prevalent for other reasons for a period of time after sobriety is achieved.

▶ **Is ADD always present after chemical abuse is controlled?**

No. Only some chemical abusers will show ADD symptoms. But remember, attentional problems are common when a person is in recovery.

◄ı◄�ı◄| **7** |►ı►ı►

The Way Out

▼

*T*here is a way out of ADD. But, remember, you won't "cure" it, for there is no cure. You won't eliminate it, for it is a lifelong condition.

What you can do is manage it. My style of therapeutic intervention—which I developed through counseling hundreds of ADD persons—is actually a mixture of education and therapy that recognizes the potential assets of ADD and the harm it has caused.

This calls for identifying ADD and accepting that you have it, working through and correcting the damage it has caused, and restructuring your life to accommodate it. Don't be ashamed of it. Face it, you probably didn't even know you had it.

◄ The Diagnosis

The first step is diagnosis. And, though diagnosis is no mean feat, I have discovered that people with ADD, once alerted to ADD's possible existence, are quite good at self-diagnosis. (If you are the least bit hesitant to undertake the task yourself, find a therapist who acknowledges the existence of adult ADD and enlist his help. (See the appendices for resources.)

The diagnosis must include a thorough childhood history. Preferably work it up with a parent, sibling, other family member, or childhood friend; they can be a marvelous aid in helping you get outside yourself and see your life from a totally different perspective.

School performance is a frequent indicator of ADD. Phrases are a dead giveaway: "If only he'd pay attention . . . ," "She's so bright, but she just doesn't finish her work," "His mind keeps wondering," or "She fidgets and wastes time."

The level of family peace often reflects the presence of an ADD child. When the ADD child was absent, things often ran more smoothly and with less turmoil. When the ADD child reappeared, disruption and chaos were not far behind—not in an ugly way, just in a frazzled way. Disciplinary and guidance methods had to be changed. Generally, more time was spent paying attention to the ADD child and more intercession with the world outside the family was necessary. Parents often were required to help the ADD child get along with friends and siblings. Memories of many fights and conflicts, uncompleted chores, and time spent focused on an overreactive son or daughter can be indicators of ADD. Many ADD children, because of their impulsivity, may have had more accidents than other children in the family. Try to recall how often the child was heard saying "I'm sorry." He really didn't mean to do wrong. He just did it. And, as though he failed to learn from experience, his childhood is likely to have been filled with repeat offenses. If you are a parent and suspect that your grown child has ADD, you may have felt that, as a child, he or she was out to get you.

In addition to an inventory of childhood history, it is also helpful to inventory a checklist of typical ADD symptoms in adults. (If you suspect that you have ADD, it will be useful to go over this list with someone close to you, because you may be unaware of your own behaviors.):

Inattention: Often fails to finish things started; often does not seem to listen; easily distracted; difficulty concentrating on sustained-attention tasks; difficulty sticking to an activity.

Impulsivity: Often acts before thinking; shifts excessively from one activity to another; has difficulty working independently; frequently talks out or interrupts; finds it difficult to wait his turn.

Hyperactivity: Excessively paces or moves; has difficulty staying seated; moves about excessively during sleep; always on the go.

Emotionality: Oversensitive to rejection and frustration; shifts moods suddenly and unexpectedly; frequent negative thinking after success or accomplishment (stemming from the belief that such success is impossible); unexplained chronic recurring depression; finds being soothed and held most difficult; needs excessive sensory input such as television or music to blot out extraneous noise.

It is useful to write down descriptive comments and anecdotes for each symptom or characteristic as you go through the assessment, and take them from both the present time and from childhood. They will help in determining the presence of ADD as well as in differentiating ADD from other conditions.

Finally, check your family history. Frequently a parent will have had ADD traits that went undiagnosed in earlier years. Sometimes it will be another family member from the previous generation. Remember, ADD tends to run in families.

◀ Self-Image

It is impossible to suffer from undiagnosed ADD without some poor living habits building up. New training is necessary so the newly diagnosed person with ADD isn't set up for failure. You can get beyond ADD, but it's imperative to make adjustments for the condition so that its effects can be nullified. You must develop a new self-image and adjust to that new self-image.

Self-images build slowly and change just as slowly. Once we get used to one, it's a bit hard to let go of it. And it feels better to hang on to a poor self-image than to strive for a good self-image because of the fear of failing to live up to a good one. If many childhood incidents have proven over and over that you are a failure or, at best, an underachiever, then your willingness to risk will be limited.

So, I ask you to:

1) Assess how you are doing now and how you've been doing (you may want to use a scale of one to five where one equals poorly, three is okay, and five superlative);

2) Make a list of traits you'd like to leave behind you. Include particular traits that cost you a lot to continue to carry. Examples include temper (blowing up under stress), blaming (accusing others for problems rather than looking at your own part in things), quitting (running away from difficult situations), and procrastination. With all of these traits, you end up losing a lot of yourself even though you gain a sense of protection—at least temporarily. (Each behavior represents a psychological attempt to protect your vulnerable feelings.)

3) Make a list of traits that you'd like to have or that you admire in others.

4) Adopt those traits. If some are made difficult by ADD, such as staying on task, commit to doing what you can do about it. Then drop responsibility for what you can't do. Take small steps.

5) Look at your new identity as someone who has ADD and is working with it. Embrace it as your own. Say goodbye to the old and reach out for the new.

And when it comes to self-image, remember, too, that having ADD is not all bad. Being a poor robot or assembly line worker means you have more time to be creative. You see the world a little bit differently than others. These are special gifts. Explore them. Just because the majority culture does things in a certain way doesn't make that way any better than yours. Exercise your way of doing things. It's important for a person with ADD to develop approaches and methods that make him feel competent.

For example, a lot is made about leaving assignments to the last minute. But does it really matter? Our culture is into planning early, but does it really matter when an assignment is started? No! It just needs to get done.

So, why not give yourself permission to start late and enjoy the doing—as long as it's done on time—instead of punishing yourself with scoldings?

Enjoy your individuality. Feel good about what you are instead of worrying about what you're not. You are you, and there is no one who's better at being that.

◀ The Group Effect

When ADD has gone undiagnosed in childhood, the initial reaction in the adult—after diagnosis—is relief: relief at finding an explanation for much of what has caused disruption and unfulfilled potential in the person's life. Euphoria may accompany the relief. Whew! It feels as if anything is possible.

At this point, it is good to talk with others about the awareness of ADD. The discussion helps ground the person until there is time to catch up with the new identity.

Most communities will have a self-help clearing house and a guide to local services. The Mental Health Association is a good place to start. Also, schools will have contacts for children with ADD. In turn, they may know whether there is an adult group. Find one of these groups and join. If no group is available locally, form your own. (See appendices for more information.)

Talk about your feelings with others in the group. First talk openly about your feelings of having a life-long condition. Begin to connect with others in the group, people who have the same characteristics you have. Realize that just as lots of people have problems with their eyesight, you share a common bond with people who have a problem with attention. Realize that you all are sensitive, probably very creative, and abused to varying degrees, depending on how well your ways were understood and tolerated as a child. Each of you will share a characteristic way of reacting to the world, and it feels really good to know that you're not alone.

Sharing experiences with the group will be quite helpful. For example, you might tell the group, "At noon, my wife asked me to mow the lawn, and I said I'd do it before she got back from the beauty shop. As she left, she mentioned she'd like to go to the movies that evening, and I said, okay. But then I spotted last week's mail on the desk, so I began to go through it. Then I got hungry and decided to go to the grocery store. On the way home I saw my friend Sam. We talked and he made me remember I'd never returned the books to the library. I was just ready to get the mower out when my wife got home. Furiously, she told me I'd ruined her evening. She'd really wanted to go to the movies. She's always blowing up. And I'm always goofing up."

Now, in order to understand the situation, the group might do a feelings analysis. Note how each person felt, starting with you. You might say something like, "I felt fine all afternoon. I had a good time and was glad to see an old friend. I was glad to see my wife and didn't mean to hurt her."

Then you would analyze your wife's feelings: "She seemed to leave in a happy mood. She even seemed happy when she first drove in the driveway, but then immediately got mad."

Now you might ask your group members to help you figure out what happened and how you can manage things better in the future.

Basically, you committed to mowing the lawn by the time your wife got home, but you didn't. And you led her to believe you'd go to a movie. From her perspective, she thought she had an agreement that would lead to the lawn being done and an entertaining evening at the movies. If you didn't want to go and had said so, she could have gotten a friend to go with her, if it was important to her.

You, in turn, meant no harm. You just got distracted. And you really want to be a nice guy, so lots of times you agree to things you're not very crazy about doing. And then it's even easier for you to get off track. And you also said "uh-huh" to your wife about the movies, perhaps wanting to please her, but forgetting you have to make such things happen. Or maybe, with the "uh-huh," you were just affirming her existence without really listening to the content of the request.

Your group will care about you. Use them to learn new ways. Learn to see yourself as you are and work to change what you don't like.

◀ Use the Word "No"

Above all, stop being the good guy unless you really want to take responsibility to follow through. It's not so bad to say "no." It's a lot easier on those around you. They may even respect you more.

If, by chance, you run into someone who won't take no for an answer, just turn the responsibility over to them, saying "I don't mean to hurt or frustrate you, but I'm not going to commit to something I may not follow through on." The other person may not like it, if that person is overly dependent on you to get his or her needs met, but you can't be responsible for that anyway, so stick to your guns. Learn to say "No!"

Use your group's help by making a commitment to say "no."
Report back each week on how well you've done this and
count on positive reinforcement from people who care and
understand.

◀ Common Questions About Getting Help

▶ **Why do people with ADD so often have negative thinking after an accomplishment?**

For one thing, most ADD people have learned
to think of themselves as inadequate. They tend
to have developed low self-esteem which makes
them think of all kinds of reasons why what
they did couldn't possibly have come because
of their capability.

Also, their negative thinking serves as a protection against someone else saying something negative first.

▶ **With the extra sensitivity that ADD people
have, how can working with a radio or TV
on help them concentrate?**

It serves as a kind of white noise, a constant
sound, that masks discrepant or irregular sounds
or sights that they would experience as more
disruptive. Also there is a consistent rhythm or
sameness to TV and radio sounds. (The technical
directors of the stations make sure that this is
true, I promise you.) The consistency soothes an
ADD person.

▶ **Does use of medication diminish the positive
traits of an ADD person, such as creativity or
the ability to synthesize information and
make unusual connections?**

No. It helps the person focus more constructively on the expression of those traits.

▶ **Can an ADD person juggle lots of things at
the same time?**

Often. In fact, it may help them to get things
done to have several things going at one time
so that they have a reason to move from one
thing to another and a specific place to put
their attention when they get bored with the
original activity. This keeps them from going
off willy-nilly.

▶ **In addition to being creative, are there other
positive traits of ADD and does it take having
ADD to have these traits?**

Traits, such as creativity and the lack of
boundary isolation that leads to cross disciplinary tendencies are only the beginning of the
positive uses for the sensitivity created by ADD.
In addition, there are interpersonal ones: empathy, sensitivity to others, the ability to see
through facades and view people and situations
as they *really* are, and an openness to sharing
thoughts and feelings.

These traits are, of course, shared by others who
do not have ADD. But the existence of ADD
gives people a built in head start.

▶ **Why would a person who finds out he has
ADD feel "as if anything is possible?"**

For one thing, it's like popping the cork on a
bottle of champagne. It flies high from having
been under pressure. The awareness of what his
problem is opens new doorways previously

closed. The ADD person has no experience in the new "world" by which to gauge limits. Time and experience will define some limits, but initially it seems that the sky's the limit.

▶ **Why would you have to teach a person with ADD to say "no," when you stated earlier that persons with ADD often say it automatically?**

Initially people with ADD say "no" as a way of buying time and power. "No" pushes the person with the request away and puts the control in the hands of the person who has ADD. Since people with ADD tend to feel intruded upon, they need such a barrier for protection.

Later, as people with ADD become socialized, they learn to be "nice guys" in order to get approval and tend to say "yes" automatically in order to please. A person with ADD needs to learn to stop and think whether he really *wants* to do something or is just trying to please or to get the person with the request off his back without making a fuss.

Saying "no" without thinking is non-constructive. Saying "no" with thought is constructive.

▶ **Sometimes my attention is better than at other times. What can I do to help myself?**

First, be kind and understanding to yourself.

Next, check to see what things may be interfering with your attention: nutrition, tiredness, stress. Ask yourself whether you have disrupted your usual schedule in any area.

Correct the disruption. Consistent structure in your life is your best friend.

▶ **What can I do to get myself to finish things I start?**

Be sure you are trying to do something that is important to you.

Give yourself an incentive to work for, promising yourself that you'll treat yourself when you complete the task. Be sure to break whatever you're doing into manageable segments and give yourself breaks along the way. But time your breaks so you keep them under control.

◂❘◀❘◀ 8 ❘▶❘▶❘▸

The Visualization Technique

▼

*T*here are those of you reading this book whose pain is indeed great from your growing-up years. Hurt, abuse, and anger—and more hurt—were so monumental you couldn't escape them, let alone do anything about them. Remember, abuse from ADD may have resulted from benign circumstances, but nonetheless it was there. A legacy remains from teachers, parents, and employers whose personal goals—to train you properly—were thwarted by the ADD and who became frustrated. The abuse may have come in the form of well-meant scoldings or behavioral limits that you couldn't abide, such as groundings or keeping you after school. Of course, at times the abuse may have been much more than that, including overreactive responses such as actual physical punishment.

For you I want to suggest that you practice a technique used in many fields for many purposes—visualization. I have, in dealing with adults diagnosed with ADD, made modifications in the technique that make it both appropriate and successful for ADD treatment. Look at it as a tool for "reparenting" yourself.

In a quiet place, sit in a comfortable chair that has arms, close your eyes, and take a step back from your experience. Think of something that makes you feel secure, very secure, safe, and protected. It might be sitting in the lap of your grandmother. Or it might be feeling the sun on your shoulder while you walk through a forest filled with the smell of springtime, a soft breeze against your cheek. Choose your own brand of safety—and feel the arm of the chair.

Imagine projecting your experience onto a movie screen, and view it as you might a movie. As you do this, grasp the arm of the chair that you're sitting in while watching the movie, and feel the security of it. You can even see yourself watching the movie.

(If you feel resistant to doing this exercise, don't do it. Your psyche is telling you: "Whoa, I'm not ready for this. It's not good for me." You may wish to do this work with a counselor or not at all. Your psyche knows best; trust it.)

Now, let's all get ready to change history.

Let your mind drift back to a time in your youth when you felt misunderstood, inadequate, out of control. Visualize that part of you in your mind's eye. You will probably feel a sensation within you that reflects how you felt at the time. Pay particular attention to that feeling, its shape, its location in your physical body, and its size and substance. Is it hot or cold, hard or soft, solid or porous? Attach a color to it.

Immediately after defining it, squeeze the arm of the chair and find that nice, warm secure feeling. As you neutralize the sensation that causes you discomfort, realize that you can grow beyond your history.

Remember, if you are projecting this experience on a movie screen, keep it there while you watch yourself sitting and watching the movie.

Next, let your mind drift back to an earlier time in your life when you encountered a similar feeling. Locate its presence in your body again and visualize where you were standing as a child when it happened. What were you doing? Squeeze the arm of the chair. Remember to keep the vision on your movie screen.

74

Now, go back and seek the earliest experience you can recall when the same constellation of events or feelings took place. You may have been four, five, or six years old. Once more, squeeze the arm of the chair and check your movie screen if you need to.

It is now time to rewrite history.

Pretend you are a script writer. You have the capability to rewrite your childhood history any way you want. You can give your child words and understanding that realistically he or she would not have had. In this rewriting job, anything is possible. Also allow the others in your drama to have words, skills, and understanding they didn't actually have but that you can give them since you are recreating their characters.

Visualize the child with the out-of-control, inadequate feelings and let the child say what he or she needs: Understanding? Support? A sense of control? Your child might say something like: "I feel overwhelmed. I need you to understand that I'm trying as hard as I can." Squeeze the arm of the chair you're sitting in. Feel it holding you up.

Visualize the grownups in the child's life reassuring the child, giving him understanding, knowledge, whatever was needed. Hear them teaching the child: "You have ADD. It's no big deal. I can help you learn to overcome its effects. You are smart. You are okay. I love you. I'm here with you and I'll help you learn to pay attention. See, you are already doing it. You're a fast learner. I love you."

If you like, feel the warm arm of the adult around the child's shoulders. Watch the adult walk the child into school and ex- plain to the teachers what is needed. See the teachers pass the message on. And see your child grow assured, secure, capable, and able to be in control.

If the adults in your early life were particularly abusive, see the child on the movie screen stop them. Have them freeze, like the child's game "Freeze," where no one can move without permission of the game leader. Let the child be the leader and call "freeze." Then let a special, understanding adult teach them about ADD.

Next, watch the abusive adults change their level of understanding, becoming enlightened. Let them say "I am so sorry. I didn't mean any harm. I didn't know any better. Please forgive me."

Watch the child on the screen take as long as he needs to do that. No rush. If the child needs to vent some anger, fine. If the child wants to scold, fine. When the feeling is vented and the child sees the adults for what they were—frightened, helpless, frustrated—forgiveness will come. But let it come in its own time as you again squeeze the arm of your chair, feeling the security it offers, the support and comfort.

Feel the child's growing sense of control. Realize that the feeling will spread and grow to be used daily as you go about your business in confidence, knowing that you are now understood and strong.

You can change each recalled experience this way. Give the child what is needed. Provide the child with the power of information and the support of understanding. Watch the child, adolescent, and adult in you grow in confidence before your mind's eye. Forgive those who hurt you out of ignorance and feel the confidence build within you to be in control of yourself as someone who has ADD. Simply make room for it when planning your activities.

◀ Dealing with Grief

In addition to the hurt and anger of abuse, you have to deal with the grief—over loss of potential—that ADD has brought into your life.

Remember that grief has several stages including denial, anger, bargaining, depression, and acceptance. Remember,

76

too, that you likely are stuck in some phase of the process of grieving and have never reached the acceptance stage. But you can.

Identify and vent your feelings. Acknowledge them to yourself—or at first just toy with the idea of them. Say them aloud to yourself and let yourself feel whatever you feel— depression, anger, denial. Then write down the feelings—and again let yourself feel whatever you feel.

Voice your feelings to someone else—a therapist, an understanding person, the group if you're in one—and let yourself feel whatever you feel. As the feelings wash through you, befriend the grieving part of you—the little boy who was so angry about feeling helpless, the young woman who felt so bad over being unable to keep the job she loved because she couldn't get the paper work done on time.

Put your arm around the part of you that needs your help. When you have released the grief, raise your head, take a deep breath of fresh air, and get ready to develop new ways to reach your potential.

◀ Common Questions About Visualization

▶ **What can I do if I can't get my mind to be quiet enough to do the visualization?**

Make sure that you get into a regular daily habit of spending time quietly so that your mind and emotions can count on the time. Make a list of intruding concerns and problems that are most likely to distract you and commit to return to them at a later time. Slow your breathing down and feel it becoming a little deeper and more regular. Experiment to see which is easiest for you, closing your eyes, keeping your eyes open, or keeping your eyes open but focusing on one thing. Clear your mind further by letting a gentle breeze carry the thoughts off or take a mental broom and sweep them aside or place them on a shelf or in a box for later sorting.

Start the visualization but don't expect to finish it. Do it in stages, being easy on yourself.

▸ **What should I do if I start feeling very emotional during the visualization?**

Stop. Don't go further into it.

Allow yourself to stay with the feeling. Be gentle and nurturing with yourself. Express the feeling out loud to yourself, letting the adult part of you realize that your little kid part was deeply touched.

You may not want to do any further work with the visualization that day. You may want to talk with someone about the feelings. Do so. Return to the visualization at a time when it feels comfortable to do so.

▸ **What do I do if I have trouble seeing pictures in my mind or don't see any at all? Does that mean there is something else wrong with me?**

There is nothing *wrong* with you. Some people visualize easily. Other people are better at hearing dialogue in their heads. And still others do best feeling things.

If you are having trouble getting pictures in your mind, try having a conversation with yourself and your inner child. Recall the conversations you had as a child, and remember what you heard that impressed you.

If this method still leaves you wanting, settle on feeling the experiences that you went through as a child and substitute the feeling you would have liked that child to have had. Bring the child feelings of joy and power. You can do this by recalling feelings of joy and power in other settings and transferring those feelings to your ADD experience.

▶ **When the history of my childhood is being rewritten, what do I do if I simply can't see my parents being helpful?**

Some people have to substitute other people for their parents. It may be an aunt or uncle, family friend, doctor, public figure, or someone from literature. Call forth the person you would have liked to have had as a parent. Some people, who are parents themselves, visualize their adult selves taking care of their child selves, saying, "I wish I'd had a parent like I am."

▶ **When I do the visualization and let myself experience the child, I get angry—very, very angry. How do I handle that?**

If you feel your anger could get out of control, protect yourself and others by doing the visualization with someone else present. A counselor can help you with this.

Often, however, we feel that any anger at all is *a lot.* This happens if we were raised with a prohibition on anger, or if we viewed a family member getting out of control with his anger. In that case, you might try feeling a little bit of it by yourself. But be kind to yourself, and call on a friend if you're concerned.

There is nothing wrong with screaming, shouting, or stomping your anger out. It's only a feeling. It's only anger. Try kicking a stone down the street, play racquetball or hand ball, throw a pillow, or say some four letter words.

▶ **Do I need to confront the people in real life who hurt me?**

No. Usually the hurt was done because of ignorance. You will be farther ahead in your healing process if you acknowledge the hurts and errors and absorb yourself in fixing them.

If your parents or teachers are open to learning, share the new information you have with them. Do this in a matter-of-fact way.

If you feel this sharing is not enough to satisfy you, then tell them how angry or hurt you were. Ask them if they realized how you felt. If they react poorly, continuing to blame or abuse you, then you may want to stand up for your inner child. Generally, however, angry confrontation is not at all necessary.

Remember, your main job is to heal yourself and take over responsibility for your growth.

▶ **Why is it so hard to forgive and go on?**

All of us have a hard time living with unfinished emotional business. Our emotions keep pulling us back to the problem in an attempt to get us to solve it. Usually we don't let go of a problem because there is some aspect that is not yet solved. People with ADD have to work hard to get past the point of hurt or blame and turn that energy into constructive action. But it's worth the effort.

▶ **How long will it take for my inner child to forgive those who abused me?**

It will take your child part as long as it needs to take. There is no point in pushing yourself. Do not let others try to tell you that you *should* forgive your abusers. It will simply happen when *all* the healing is done.

▶ **What if I can't get my child to forgive them?**

Often unexpressed anger stands in the way of being able to forgive someone. This is most likely to happen when we understand what happened to us but have not yet fully felt or acknowledged all the feelings within us. It's a matter of getting what we know cognitively to the level of feelings. Once the feelings are fully acknowledged and felt, and appropriate action is taken on behalf of them, the forgiveness will come.

▶ **How long will it take me to go through the grief process?**

Grieving also takes as long as it takes. A major grief reaction (to a divorce or death of a loved one) takes at least two years.

Recovery from the grief over your lost potential will go much more quickly, provided you work with it. Doing the visualization work will facilitate your recovery, and it may only take a session or two to get beyond the feelings you've carried all these years.

▶ **What does it mean if I don't or can't feel any grief over my lost potential?**

You may have already gone through your grief. You certainly don't want to make up feelings you don't have.

▶ **How can I learn to let myself feel?**

Begin with another person who will help you realize when you are feeling. That person can be a counselor but doesn't necessarily have to be. She can be a friend who will stop you when you get an expression on your face or act in a way that tells her you are having strong feelings. You can then learn to identify what you are feeling.

▶ **If I start letting myself feel, will I still be able to work and stay in control of my life?**

Of course. In fact, you will be in even more control because it is an illusion that your feelings will go away if you don't acknowledge them. They actually only get more out of your control, doing their work behind the scenes.

To protect other areas of your life from the effects of your feelings, you can assign specific times to pay attention to them and to pay attention to work. Let your inner child know you will come back to the feelings at that specific time.

▶ **I'm shy in groups and wouldn't want to let other people know what I really feel. Can I fix myself in private?**

You can begin to work with your feelings in private, but ultimately you will need to openly acknowledge them. Being reticent to share feelings openly is one of the symptoms of the hurt and emotional damage you have suffered. Shame is one of the most common reactions to such hurt, leaving us feeling *as if* others would reject us or not want to be around us if they really knew what we felt or were like. Not so!

82

▶ **I get disgusted with myself for being so disorganized. What can I do to help myself?**

First of all, quit being so abusive with yourself. You learned that as a child, and it's time to unlearn it. Realize why you are so disorganized, do what you can to improve, and then realize that disorganization is not a mortal sin. It's just an inconvenience.

If all else fails, hire someone to keep track of your stuff or make a trade with someone who needs a skill you have.

▶ **If I don't feel comfortable doing the visualization, how can I feel better about myself?**

There are many ways to heal the past so you can move on to the future. You may be able to write out your healing. Try writing a letter to the child within you who suffered the repercussions of ADD. Also write letters to those who hurt you and to those who helped you. You can get your anger out this way and can even write a letter forgiving everyone involved, but only when you are good and ready.

I've known people who painted out their healing and others who used athletics, music, and drama. Anything goes. Use the mode that you feel drawn to.

▶ **Will the visualization conflict with what my counselor is having me do?**

I can't imagine how it would, regardless of the type of counseling you are undergoing. However, check with that person. He or she may even be able to help you visualize better.

▶ **How can I like the child part of me? She's so dumb.**

You have a good case of self-abuse going. Realize you learned to feel that way and so you can unlearn it. Try getting a picture of yourself when you were about five or six. That's probably when you started school and began to have trouble with your ADD. Talk with the child in the picture.

Share the picture with someone you trust. Often a therapist can help you with this phase, especially if you have a tough case of "dumb feeling." As the other person loves your child, you will have a model to watch and imitate. The day will come, mark my words, when you will appreciate your child and understand the pain she's been through. You will then look at her as a courageous person who survived.

▶ **I can't get over feeling bad about having trouble in school and everyone blaming me.**

The most common block in this kind of situation is unexpressed anger. Call the people who offended you into your mind, and let the school child tell them off royally. Then, visualize the child going through school successfully, with understanding from the adults and other children. In fact, have them congratulate you on your assets while helping you cope with your ADD.

That ought to do the trick.

◄ ◄ ◄ 9 ► ► ►

Restructuring

▼

Learning to successfully live with your ADD means not only repairing the emotional damage it has caused you, but also learning to manage your behavior to reflect your new self-image and to accomplish your new goals. Generally this means unlearning some old, bad habits and structuring your life and thinking to promote new ones. Controlling your temper, managing your time, and completing assigned tasks are top priorities. Here are ways to help you achieve follow-through, stick to an activity, handle distractions, reach the goals you set, and generally meet your special needs in both your personal world and the workplace:

◄ Cutting a Deal

Follow-through has been tough for you, since distractions pull you off course. In relationships, lack of follow-through destroys trust. Rarely have you meant to hurt others, but that is the effect nonetheless.

You'll find it helpful to cut a deal with anyone you're involved with, especially on a personal level, since you are likely to let down in the comfort of your personal life. Ask for reminders saying you really intend to follow through but tend to get off track, over-schedule, and under-organize. Also, take extra responsibility to remind yourself. You may add personal items to your appointment book, mount a sign on your refrigerator, or do whatever works for you. Lists and schedules can be your best friends.

It's important to agree only to what you want to do. With your sensitivity, it's difficult for you to fake it effectively. You need to be honest.

◀ Pacing

It's a good idea for you to break each job into small, manageable segments that fit your attention span. For example, the yard may need to be mowed in three stages. In stage one, pick up all the things laying about, and then take a break to do whatever else you want for a short time. Then, in stage two, ready the lawn mower, which may include getting the gas for it. Give yourself a break to do something not connected to the lawn, such as watching a TV show that has a clear ending time. This will be the time to return to work on the lawn. In stage three, mow the lawn. If it's a large lawn, mow it in sections according to a prearranged plan, taking a break between each section.

By structuring your breaks to fit your own timing, you are killing two birds with one stone: you're respecting your natural ability and you are putting yourself in charge of meeting your needs. Be sure you limit your breaks. You may want to get a timer. Or limit yourself to watching one half-hour TV show, or listening to one segment of a radio talk show, or reading one article in the newspaper. You may want to limit yourself to performing a single chore on the break—putting in the laundry or making a casserole for dinner.

No matter what the task, pacing is crucial for you. There is absolutely no point in pressing yourself to stick to a task. It's a better idea—and one that carries better odds for completing the task—to take a break when needed and as often as needed, and then go back to the task at hand. When control is in your hands, over time there will be an increase in attention to the task.

86

◀ Work Space

Develop a good relationship with your work area. Being pinned down in a small space with no ability to move about is a problem for most people with ADD. On the other hand, your need for structure and limits remains important. So, to accommodate both needs, I suggest a moderate size work space that allows opportunities to move in and out easily. It should be separated from the surrounding environment so that it blocks out noise and keeps visual distractions to a minimum. Cubicles work well. Separate rooms are good. The worst environment for you, in all likelihood, is a large, noisy room with no barriers to screen out the environment.

◀ Movement

It's helpful for you to be able to move from one area of work to another during your time-out periods. It will help with the fidgets that likely affect you after you sit too long. This is one reason for taking breaks. If you're trapped in a lecture hall, take an end seat so you can get up and get a drink of water. It's also a good idea to have something to keep your hands busy.

◀ Sound

Sound screens are important. That's why having the TV or radio on in the background may be advantageous. At first it may seem like a distraction, but in reality, if the TV or music forms a kind of "white noise" with an even level of intensity, it actually covers up discrepant noises that can be a distraction. The hum of a ceiling fan or motor can do wonders to soothe and focus you.

Bottom line to your work environment: Allow yourself the freedom to work in the environment that feels best to you. Forget the guidelines generally taught in school or by parents. Your intuition knows better.

◀ Planning

You probably feel better, more secure, and capable of accomplishment by having a set pattern, at least for certain tasks. When I think of the way my son has learned to plan tasks, I'm always reminded of the pre-flight check that pilots go through before taking an airplane off the ground. They never deviate from the specific checklist and automatically adhere to it to provide safety for their passengers and themselves. Such patterned behavior may suit you very well. I strongly recommend integrating such patterns into every ordinary task, whether it's closing up the house at night or bathing the baby. It's important that you make up your own sequences, though, so they fit you.

A planner
sequence

◀ Mastering Distractions

Procrastination traditionally has been considered a fear or rebellion response: fear of failure or rebellion against a teacher, parent, or someone who pressed us to do something we didn't want to do.

But we're not dealing with tradition here. We're dealing with ADD. Yes, while you may be more susceptible to the fear of failure because you've had more experience with it, and you may have found yourself a rebel, there's an additional reason why you may *appear* to procrastinate: distractibility.

You can change that, for delivering the goods on time is part of your new self-image, isn't it?

It's crucial for you to have an outline for any project and—preferably—an appointment book or daily schedule with the patterns for work clearly laid out.

Despite a lot of talk to the contrary, ADD people are really no different from anyone else when it comes to avoiding work they don't want to do but feel they should. You may be hit harder by it than your fellow heel-draggers, though, because it's characteristically much more difficult for you to concentrate on something you don't want to do (remember, this is one of the diagnostic criteria). But, to live in this world, you must commit to doing some of these "should" tasks. Make them part of your own agenda.

If the checkbook needs to be balanced, it's important to know what the advantages are for doing the balancing. Then check for an inner willingness to take on the job as something that is in your best interest—not because someone says it ought to be done. If you can't find a reason, then don't do it: hire someone to do it, or trade with your partner or spouse for another task.

Leave more time to get distracted—often. That's one way. But I also recommend leaving a shorter time to finish a project, carefully and thoroughly structuring the time, and then going for broke. In other words, let yourself procrastinate. The condensed time frame will make you focus more intensely on the project, and all extraneous activities can be let go—whew! No dishes or yard work allowed.

It works. One of my patients and I structured her school semester as the chart on the next page shows. Just as I helped her, you may wish to have a buddy help you. The chart came about with four weeks left in the term. Five papers were due, six exams were coming up, and she still had to attend classes. As you can see, even though we eliminated all unnecessary activities, we still scheduled some TV time. The reward was 17 credits of straight A's for my client. I rest my case! I have included other sample charts as well.

◀ Getting Your Temper Under Control

The earlier temper control is begun, the easier it is to effect alternative ways for its management. A temper is something that lives only through reinforcement. It can be controlled in the child if the child is taught to find other means to get his or her needs met. But, because that rarely happens, let's pick up on the adult level, learning how to break the temper cycle.

DAILY ACTIVITY SCHEDULE

NAME: Jane Sample _____ DATE: _____

DESCRIPTION: full time student (straight A record) who works 8 hrs per week

	MONDAY	TUESDAY	WEDNESDAY	THURSDAY	FRIDAY	SATURDAY	SUNDAY
7:00 am	Pack Lunch Eat, Watch TV	Pack Lunch, Eat	Pack Lunch Eat, watch TV	Pack Lunch Eat	Pack Lunch Eat, watch TV	TV or sleep in work	Eat Lightly Read Book
8:00 am	Drive time	Drive to school Study at school	Drive time	Drive to school Study at school	Drive Time		Alcoholics Anonymous
9:00 am	Physical Education		Physical Education		Physical Education		
10:00 am	Change Clothes 10:15 school Counselor	Lab 10:30-History	Change Clothes Errands	LAB 10:30-History	Change Clothes Errands		10:30-Lunch
11:00 am	Lab		Lab		Lab	Shopping and Chores	
12:00 noon	Logic	Sociology	Logic	Sociology	Logic		Study or Library
1:00 pm	1:30-Spanish	1:30-English	1:30 Spanish	1:30 English	1:30-Spanish	Library and Computer time with breaks	and Computer Time with
2:00 pm			Drive Time		Free	as long as needed	breaks
3:00 pm	3:30-Snack	Study	3:30-Counsellor	Library	Time		
4:00 pm	Study		Drive Time 4:30-Freetime	Drive Time work			
5:00 pm				Drive time			Dinner with a friend
6:00 pm	Dinner Drive	Dinner and Drive time	Dinner	Dinner		Dinner with friends	6:30 Plan next week
7:00 pm	Study with walking breaks		Study	Study		a movie or hang out	Finish study projects
8:00 pm		Alcoholics Anonymous					
9:00 pm	Watch TV	Drive time					
10:00 pm	Bed and Relaxation Time	Bed and relaxation time	10:30-Bed and relaxation time	10:30 Bed and relaxation time	Bed and relaxation time	10:30 Bed and relaxation time	Bed and relaxation time
11:00 pm				time		time	
12:00 midnight							

5/7 - 5/11

5/14 - 5/21

Mon
10:30 And.
1p Station
6:30 Aerobics

Books
2 Good 4 Dim Good
Fight D Bank
Wake Up Sleep
32 Elephant kennels

Tues 9a Hair

1p WSRT
600-0000

Call Bob @ Network

6:30p Aerobics

Wed
12n Meeting w/ producer
1p Station
Send card to boss (ratings)

Thurs. 7:30 - 8 Firestone
8:45 Breakfast
12n P/u car
1p Station

Fri
11:30 Mike J.
1p Station
6:30 Aerobics
Sat 1p John - Hair
Call producer

Mon
1p Station
5p Lee Bennett - Baker

Tues
8:30 And.
Call John A @ 611-1111
1p Station

Wed
1p Station

Thurs
1p Station

Fri
1p Station

91

MONTHLY PLANNER   Preferred by a 35 year old male salesman.

MONTH __Sept.__

MONDAY	TUESDAY	WEDNESDAY	THURSDAY	FRIDAY	SATURDAY	SUNDAY
	☺ Dancing	Pay bills		☺ Lunch with mother		yard
Work Project due	☺ Dancing		Community meeting		Work	Work
	☺ Dancing	Pay bills		prepare work for trip		PACK / Leave
Out of town →				☺ John's 10th b day party		yard
write	☺ Dancing	write	Write	Turn in written proposal	Dinner/ Theatre boss	

DAILY ACTIVITY SCHEDULE

NAME:_____   DATE:_____

DESCRIPTION:_____

	MONDAY	TUESDAY	WEDNESDAY	THURSDAY	FRIDAY	SATURDAY	SUNDAY
7:00 am							
8:00 am							
9:00 am							
10:00 am							
11:00 am							
12:00 noon							
1:00 pm							
2:00 pm							
3:00 pm							
4:00 pm							
5:00 pm							
6:00 pm							
7:00 pm							
8:00 pm							
9:00 pm							
10:00 pm							
11:00 pm							
12:00 midnight							

Remember, that temper gets a particular hold on ADD people because of the tendency for emotional flooding to occur. So, step one is: never try to deal with a temper when it is active. Make plans when all is calm, cool, and collected. Acknowledge that you have a temper. Forget the business of blaming others. To be sure, someone cutting in front of you on the freeway may have triggered your anxiety, surprised you, or frightened you, but your particular reaction of temper is *your* responsibility. You must realize that there are other ways to react to the stress. And with your willingness, you can learn alternatives that work particularly well for you in dealing with family and work settings, the places where temper is most likely to work against you.

1) Decide on a signal that means it's time to stop whatever is going on. In our house, it's the "time out" sign used in sports. Anyone in the family can use it and we automatically stop— no questions asked. The questions can come later. This time-out breaks into the flooding and stops the emotions from taking over. Practically, this type of thing will work in a family setting, but what about when someone pulls in front of you in traffic? What do you do then? Pull your car over to the side of the road if necessary. If you're at the office, take a walk if you can, or go to the restroom and wash your face. Go outside. The point is, *stop the emotional flooding*. Tell your partner, "I'm going to read for a while." If others are around, tell them you'll be back in a little while. Go to the store for milk if you have to. If it is your partner who's having the trouble, be nonchalant with other people and just say, "He's taking a break." No one will notice if the emotional level is held down.

2) Identify the feeling underlying the anger—fear, frustration, helplessness, hopeless—and use words to express that feeling.

"I feel helpless in this situation."

"I felt frightened when that car pulled out in front of me."

"I feel put down by you."

Be honest. It may be hard at first, but it pays off once you've learned to do it. Start by making the statements to yourself, if it's too difficult to do so with others initially.

3) Ask yourself two simple questions: "What do I need to feel better or become a winner here? How can I get it?"

4) Give yourself permission to get whatever it is you want (certainly within socially acceptable limits). Power in a situation is a common need, and you must take it to get your needs met.

5) Promise yourself that you will continue to work to get what you want without throwing a temper tantrum.

6) Congratulate yourself on a job well done.

You'll be surprised how quickly you can break the temper cycle by following these steps. It is not a long, trying process—unless someone around you enables you to continue with your temper or even cultivates it by reinforcing it. They do you no favor but probably don't know any better, so you might as well make up your mind to open up alternatives in spite of them.

Every time someone gives in to your temper, you end up a loser. Every time someone scolds you or gives any attention to your temper, you end up a loser. You're no loser, so stop giving your power away to others. Get it through your head that you're a winner and deserve to be one.

What do you do, though, if you are waiting on a customer and he becomes angry and unfairly challenges you? A person with ADD's first reaction would be to fight back. But that's definitely nonconstructive for business. So you need a quick-fix technique—a way to deflect your anger immediately and keep it from escalating until you have the time to sort yourself out and follow the steps above. Try a stop-review-go approach to such situations:

Put a "stop" sign where you can see it—a sticker on the cash register, say, or a little trinket on your watchband. When something happens, glance at it and visualize yourself stopping your temper, as you would a car at an intersection. Use the sports time-out sign if you want.

Quickly, during this mental pause, look over a couple of acceptable options to blowing your top or striking out. It could be just a smile and an offer to get the manager, or an offer to help the customer put the complaint in writing. Once you've begun collecting options to temper as you retrain yourself, they will come rather quickly.

Now, go ahead and release yourself to exercise the option you chose.

◀ Common Questions About Restructuring

▶ **How do I quit taking the lack of follow-through by my friend with ADD personally? It makes me feel as if the person doesn't really care about me.**

Your reaction is very normal. To overcome it, use your brain to begin to change how you feel. Realize mentally that the lack of follow-through is a symptom of ADD. Talk to yourself, saying, "It's not me that's causing the problem. My friend *does* care about me." It will take a little time, but I would expect your feelings to listen. If they don't, then you probably felt uncared for as a child, and this behavior by your friend is triggering old memories that you need to work with.

▶ **If I agree to only what I want to do, my wife calls me selfish. And I feel selfish. Isn't it wrong to be selfish?**

Selfishly eating the last piece of cake without sharing it with others in the room is quite different from taking care of yourself. I'm talking about taking responsibility for getting your own needs met. If you will do that, then you will be in a much better place to take care of others who truly cannot take care of themselves, such as people who are sick, or children.

To consistently do for another person what they can do for themselves cheats them of the wonderful reward of being responsible. You wouldn't want to do that, would you?

▶ **It makes me mad to have trouble keeping my attention on a job. What can I do about my bad feelings?**

Acknowledge to yourself that it is a nuisance having to accommodate your ADD. Get those feelings out. Then, congratulate yourself for doing the job.

Say, "There goes that ADD of mine again." Then laugh and say, "And I'm beating it. Good for me."

▶ **Isn't being controlling a bad way to be?**

Being controlling has earned a bad name these days. A controlling person tries to control what other people do as well as the outcomes of

97

anything he or she is involved with. That's not the same as being *in control.*

To be *in control* means we are able to take responsibility for ourselves and our behavior, neither blaming others nor circumstances for our difficulties or inadequacies. We also know when we are incapable of accomplishing whatever we desire and we purposely let go of control, at least for a period of time. There is a conscious, thought-through decision, taking into account all information at our disposal, before we decide to change our pathway or even quit.

There is nothing bad about being *in control.*

▶ **If I have to sit and listen during meetings at work, it makes me feel awful trying to stay still. I feel like I want to jump out of my skin but I need to look professional. What can I tell my boss or colleague if I take in something to keep my hands busy?**

Simply say you concentrate better when your hands are occupied and leave it at that.

▶ **Why does playing with a hand-held water toy help me stay still?**

It gives you something to focus your attention on almost hypnotically. By doing this, you are less likely to be distracted by other things that are going on around you. It is soothing to the nerves and allows you to focus on the main agenda.

▶ **Which kind of chart should I use to keep track of my time?**

Different people with ADD respond to different types of charts. You will need to experiment. If you use one that is highly structured, it is important that you be the one to decide what goes into it rather than have someone else tell you what should be there. Some people do better starting each day with a blank page and making a list of what is to be done.

▶ **My spouse has an awful temper but blames me for causing it. What can I do to avoid triggering it? Is there anything I can do to take the steam out of his temper if he won't work on it?**

When you two are in a calm mood, ask him what hurt him. Then, practice saying things in a matter-of-fact way. Know, however, that he needs to take responsibility for his display of temper.

Do not reinforce his temper. When he blasts off, do not argue. The most you want to say is, "I'll talk with you when you're calm." You may need to wait until he is calm to say this.

Most people with tempers will display just as much temper as they can get away with. So, if you don't like the temper outbursts, tell him you are simply unwilling to put up with them. Tell him what will happen when he allows his temper to get out of control. You might say, "When you yell, I'm going to leave the house. I'll return when you speak in a normal voice." Then, you must be willing to follow through. You will find that you can set the limit anywhere you want and, if you mean it, the person will adjust his behavior.

▶ **I used to have a temper but it is much better now that I've been working on it. My husband still reacts as if I have one though, tiptoeing**

around on eggshells. How can I get him to stop?

Ask him, "What will it take to get you to relax? I've changed and I need you to catch up with my changes." Do realize, though, that it may take several months for him to catch up. It won't happen all in one day, either. So some patience on your part is wise. On the other hand, if your husband continues to walk on eggshells, you may need to set a limit on his behavior by saying, "Hey, cut it out. I'm getting turned off. I'm even beginning to wonder whether you want my temper back."

▶ **Are there certain circumstances when an ADD person's temper will be more likely to erupt even after control measures have been learned?**

Tiredness is the biggest culprit I know. Also, keep track of the amount of stress that you are under. Times of change are high stress times and likely circumstances for an explosion.

◄ ◄ ◄ **10** ► ► ►

For Family and Friends

▼

My heart goes out to parents who are frustrated beyond words, trying to get their offspring to act responsibly.

We all lose it at times, berating our sons and daughters out of our own sense of helplessness, but for parents of an ADD child, the trials are particularly painful and frustrating. Believe me, I know.

ADD will keep parents from having the kind of child they expect and want. We parents are under terrific peer pressure to have our children, as an extension of ourselves, perform up to cultural standards, and we often pass the pressure on to our kids. We expect them to produce so we can feel acceptable. We make them responsible for our achievements as parents.

As if that's not enough, we expect them to achieve by being taught in a particular way. Heaven help the child with ADD who cannot readily screen out external stimuli. He is still placed in a classroom with twenty-five or more other kids and told it's his responsibility to pay attention.

Ideally, we won't permit such abuse—and we won't commit it, either. If we had known of the ADD, we would have evaluated the child in light of all his skills and limitations and then provided an environment supportive of the child's needs so blossoming could occur. Our job—to ignore peer pressure and prepare an environment that is supportive of growth—would have been carried out with care and love. Most of us never did this.

Leave your guilt behind. You did the best you could. But realize any adult child will need help to overcome the repercussions of the abuse. Even lack of understanding is perceived as abuse, as I'm using the term.

It's crucial to realize that a person is not bad because he has a temper outburst, is unable to stick to a task, or impulsively changes plans. It's a nuisance to live with these behaviors, but we must distinguish between the person and the behavior. None of us is so perfect that we can stand in judgment of others. What we can do is say "no" to behaviors. We can even reject behaviors while understanding the source of them.

A simple response like, "I understand you're angry, but, no, you may not hit me," seems like no more than common sense, but in fact reflects a good deal of self-control and understanding.

◀ Parenting Your ADD Child

The trick to completing the childrearing process of an ADD young adult is fairly simple, if a few rules are followed:

1) Intervene with the outside world on behalf of the ADD child as much as is needed when the child is young, and then slow down each year.

2) Similarly, give your ADD child increasing responsibility with each year and let him know you believe he can handle it.

3) Let go of your dreams for your son's or daughter's potential. Instead, seek to uncover his or her dreams. Then support them. Just because

102

your ADD child shows natural ability with numbers doesn't mean he can or would want to become an accountant. Quit pushing and let him use his number skills to become a top-notch salesperson, or whatever he *wants* to become.

4) Let your ADD young adult follow a creative path toward adulthood. Just because everyone else in the family has a college degree doesn't mean your grown child has to have one, too. Let go. I'm not saying persons with ADD can't make it in college but only that the decision needs to fit the person.

5) Give your child your belief in his ability to do well by and for himself. Not only is such belief a precious gift, it also sets up a greater likelihood of success.

6) If your adult ADD child is acting irresponsibly or destructively, let him suffer the consequences of his actions. You don't need to get into punishing him for misdeeds or irresponsibility. Rather, simply allow natural consequences to fall where they may. Do not bail your son or daughter out of trouble. Stand by his side, however, while he bails himself out of trouble. For example, don't have your attorney get your child out of a DWI charge. Instead, offer to help him get help. Go to court with him, or be available to talk and plan if your child wishes. Go to Al-Anon and give him the AA number. But don't be a pest on any of the issues. Make the offer; then back off.

Parenting the adult ADD child is simple in concept but tough in execution because you must overcome your own weaknesses and vulnerabilities. You have to learn to say "no" and be willing to let go of control. He may do things differently than you would have, but who says your way is right for everyone?

If you are having difficulty being firm, you may want to ask a friend to give you some help. If you start to weaken, say, in response to a request for money, call your friend and say, "I'm thinking of giving him more money." Your friend can take you out to lunch until the urge passes.

◀ Parents, Siblings, and ADD

Realistically, brothers and sisters will fuss and fight to some degree. But ADD often multiplies the conflicts, sometimes unbearably, and complicates the sibling relationships to the extent that special effort must be made to keep balance and harmony amongst brothers and sisters. A few simple—and not so simple—strategies for parents to follow when children are young:

1) Basically ignore their antics unless one sibling consistently takes advantage of the other. There is a good deal more sibling abuse— verbal, sexual, and physical—than meets the eye, and it occurs when one sibling characteristically takes advantage of the other. How do you tell what's really going on? You may need to play detective to decide. Do a bit of eavesdropping, like a fly on the wall. Listen to both sides of the story, and be careful that the more articulate, calmer person isn't the one believed all the time.

2) Set up situations where cooperation reaps more rewards than conflict does. For example, walk away from them when they begin to argue; pay attention and praise them when they cooperate.

3) Expect one sibling to behave better than the other for periods of time and then expect the

104

roles to be reversed. This is just a normal part of daily living. Even though one may have ADD and will often have special needs, the other—the so-called normal one—will behave as a normal child, with good days and bad days. Just because one child has ADD doesn't mean the other is a saint.

4) Teach each child to use words to tell you what he wants. Help the ADD child who is impulsive learn to take time to get the words out and take time to get his needs met. And how do you do that? By showing him that words work. Be very patient. Wait for the child to speak his piece; take time to understand what he's trying to say.

5) Teach the children how each person is different—not better or worse. And teach them how they can use their differences to help one another if they cooperate. Teach them what ADD is and how it works.

6) Reinforce how families stick together to help one another, and how brothers and sisters can fuss sometimes but still respect each other's differences.

◀ Adult Siblings and ADD

Now let's suppose this ground work had not been laid. It's never too late to learn. As they get older, one sibling can approach the other and begin to get acquainted.

The one with ADD may want to share the new information being learned, for once the condition of ADD is identified, they can both talk about the condition rather than the person.

It's a nuisance to have ADD, and it's a nuisance to live with a person with Attention Deficit Disorder. Siblings shared hard

105

times from different sides of the table. Each sibling may want to share feelings, even grieve together a little, for both lost a "normal" sibling relationship to ADD. Each can share what he or she likes about the other's skills, what's admired and respected. They might agree on a cue, like the time-out signal, to be used when either sibling is getting frustrated. (We're assuming here that all parties have been informed of the ADD and believe in it, which, of course, is part of your job as a successful family leader.)

Don't get me wrong. ADD will still be a factor. Personality differences may still make it difficult for siblings to work together. But reconciling over the ADD does bring understanding and empathy, and don't underestimate the power of understanding: It supports love.

◀ Try Negotiating

Blaming can be such a large part of an ADD person's life—and the lives of those who live with him—that learning negotiating skills is not only desirable but necessary.

Whether you are a friend, parent, spouse, or ADD person, follow these guidelines:

- ◀ Remember that it doesn't matter *why* something happened.

- ◀ But it does matter *what* happened.

- ◀ Therefore, eliminate all judgment from your discussions. (Later, you can work on eliminating judgment from your thoughts, too.)

- ◀ Get to the facts.

- ◀ Come up with a plan to solve the problem rather than worry how the problem got there. Be specific in your plan.

106

◀ Lay out specific ways to accomplish the steps in your plan.

◀ Set the plan in motion, one step at a time, and stick to it at all costs. You'll get used to negotiating your needs, and you will end up feeling like, and being, a winner in the long run.

As explained in the previous chapter, follow-through is tough for someone with ADD, since distractions have the effect of pulling them off course. In relationships, lack of follow-through destroys trust. Rarely does an ADD person mean to hurt you, but that is the effect nonetheless. The point is: Don't take lack of follow-through personally. It's only a symptom of ADD, not lack of caring or love.

Whether you are the ADD person or the person who lives with him, it is helpful to negotiate a deal, since the comfort of closeness in a relationship is likely to lead to a let-down in diligence. We all often behave the worst around those we love the most.

Ask for permission to issue reminders. (Don't just assume them as your right.) The person reminding should recognize that the ADD person sincerely intends to follow through but should also recognize the tendency to get off-track. Both you and the ADD person have to take extra responsibility in this. Bearing in mind that lists and schedules can be the ADD person's best friends, you might help in posting them, making sure they're up to date, and, with the agreement of the ADD person, seeing that they're adhered to. (It's best if the ADD person himself makes the lists. Personal experience has taught me that this is the most effective way for lists to work.)

Be sure, if you are the spouse, friend, or parent of an ADD person, that you depersonalize the experience and that you omit anger from your interaction. A tall order? You bet, and one that takes practice to deliver. But you can do it, once your expectations come in line with the reality of ADD. It won't be immediate, but once you've relinquished your need to have your expectations met (and who said they weren't loaded with your own dysfunctions?), you can reassure the ADD person that it's okay to say "no" if the person doesn't want to do whatever you ask. The next time your ADD person says "no" to your request, say a big "thank you" for his being honest.

When there is a lack of follow-through in a particular situation, nicely and gently be sure that "yes" was intended when the commitment was made. If "yes" remains the answer, then ask "when" again in an anger-free tone. Or—maybe—ask "how" the person intends to follow through. Set a time line acceptable to both of you. If the time elapses without the ADD person completing the task, do it yourself—be it finding a companion for a movie or mowing the lawn—rather than becoming bitter or resentful.

Continuing to try to get someone to follow through only leads to frustration and, frankly, it's important once the negotiation stage has passed to simply remember to stop expecting follow-through. Don't start from this point, but do end at this point if practice doesn't lead to success.

For the ADD person, there are ramifications and responsibilities to the negotiation process. After reassurances that only commitments will be made where the follow-through is intended, it's very important that the ADD person indeed follow through. The willingness to try must be negotiated once and for all. Individual situations must be negotiated as needed. There are times, even when you try your best with an ADD person, when they fail to follow through. And if they fail, don't blame yourself for permanent damage to trust in the relationship. Of course, it may not mean loss of the relationship entirely, but no one will blame you for seeing him—or her—as someone who cannot be trusted to live up to commitments.

Grief on your part over that loss is common and, in fact, some of the anger that occurs is a part of the grief reaction.

108

◀ Dealing with Rigidity

The sensitivity of ADD people makes them prone to shut down or overreact in pressure or surprise situations. And the surprises don't have to be unpleasant ones. I remember well one birthday when I thought it would be fun to put special candles on the cake of an ADD person—candles that couldn't be blown out. I didn't know at the time that the person had ADD and, anyway, wouldn't have expected the result I got, which was anger, at the surprise and at me. I didn't understand at the time why my attempt to bring fun to the party backfired. Now I understand.

To say with a sharp agitated voice, "Quick, we're late. I just looked at my watch and we're already late," is to court resistance and irritation. The ADD person is likely to look at you with disdain or even anger. The more you prod, force, or become hysterical, the more he will resist.

So, difficult as it may be, force yourself to be calm. Explain the situation. In fact, asking the ADD person calmly for help is much more likely to yield a positive response. It may take a few more minutes in the beginning—and tons more effort on your part—but the results in the long term will more than offset your initial frustration. Don't worry if you slip up sometimes. I know how it feels because I get scared and frantic sometimes, and in so doing become my own worst enemy in dealing with my ADD son. Forget your errors, for they are part and parcel of living, and strive simply to do the best you can. It's a tall order, but you can do it.

◀ Living

Living with someone who has ADD takes lots of understanding on both sides, much ability to trust in one another's best intentions, and lots of negotiation skills. As long as each person is good of heart, and willing to take responsibility, letting the other work on himself, the relationship has a good prognosis. If one person needs to be over-controlling or particularly

109

needs to keep the ADD person inadequate, then a healthy relationship is a lot less likely. The merits of the relationship need to be reconsidered under these circumstances.

Quality relationships can survive—and flourish—when there are two winners and no losers. This takes seeing the other's point of view, communicating an understanding of that viewpoint, and seeking a resolution without stopping until you find a mutually suitable solution that you both can live with. Good luck, and keep at it until you find the answer.

◀ Common Questions from Friends and Family Members

▶ **I feel very guilty about what we did and allowed to be done to our son when he was a child. Is there anything we can do to feel better? And what can we do for our son?**

For yourself, please be forgiving. Know that you did the very best you could do at the moment you were doing it. Had you known a better way, you'd have used it.

For your son, sit down with him and tell him of your new awareness. Give him information. Tell him you think he did a tremendous job surviving thus far and that you would like to support him. And you might want to help him get some relearning if he would like to. There's nothing wrong with including financial support for schooling or retraining, if he requests it or accepts your offer accompanied with a plan and follow-through.

Don't overdo to make up for the past. Don't take responsibility to fix him now because you feel guilty. Rather, form a partnership with him in which he does all he can do and you help out where you can. You may want a counselor to help you determine where the line between helping and enabling lies.

▶ **Why does my ADD husband get all his jobs done at work and fail to get anything finished at home? He's either a couch potato watching TV or he's asleep.**

It is not unusual for adults with ADD to use up all their energy focusing their attention at work. By the time they get home, there's no energy left for goal directed behavior.

Don't take his behavior personally or think he doesn't care. Talk with him about setting aside a specific time, after a rest, to do one thing at a time. Let him know it would really help you.

It also might be a great help to do some chores together. Team work often is effective in helping the ADD person stay centered on an activity.

▶ **Why do I have to renegotiate every little situation with my spouse? Is she just pretending to agree with me to get me off her back?**

In all likelihood not. It's important to determine whether your wife intends to cooperate with you and simply forgets or gets distracted or whether she is indeed just agreeing to get you off her back.

You must make it safe for her to be honest with you, which includes saying "no." Tell her that and make sure the next "no" is greeted with, "I'm glad you're telling me when you don't want to do something."

111

▶ **From the sound of things, my non-diagnosed adult ADD son married a non-diagnosed adult ADD woman. I've never understood how they can have such verbal uproars and then make up in a little while. What can they do?**

Very possibly their uproars bother you more than them. Theirs is a common pattern when two people with ADD find each other. It's wonderful or awful. But remember, they probably understand each other on a very deep level, because of their shared condition. They would, though, both benefit from some counseling to find other ways to communicate that might be less emotionally charged. But that has to be left up to them.

▶ **What is the likelihood that they will have an ADD child?**

Fairly good. The research is not in yet, so I can't give you a definitive answer. They would, however, do well to acquire some skills before they bring a child into the situation, ADD or not.

▶ **Why is it better if the person with ADD makes up the reminder's list?**

Because a person with ADD feels everything acutely, he does better to be in control of what affects him. Making up that list puts the power in the right hands.

▶ **How do I "depersonalize" my experience trying to negotiate with someone with ADD?**

◀ Use your brain instead of your feelings.

◀ Think about what is happening.

◀ Think about what you would like to happen.

◀ Be aware of your expectations.

112

◀ Be aware of what you are feeling: fear, frustration, helplessness.

◀ Take responsibility for your feelings and learn what you need to do in order to attend to them.

◀ Enter your negotiations with a clear mind and settled feelings.

▶ **I'm sick and tired of making all the adjustments to my spouse's ADD. What options do I have?**

Sounds like you need to do some self-nurturing and spend extra time getting your needs met. You may have been depending on him or her too much and ended up out in the cold. Though you can understand your spouse's ADD, you do not have to acquire the condition.

Be a bit more selfish. For example: Let's say your family has decided to have a garage sale. You ended up with the job of labeling all the items even though you hate doing it. But you took the job because you were afraid it wouldn't get done if left to your distractible ADD spouse. You want to be able to talk to the people coming by, too, instead of doing the awful job. My advice to you is drop the labeling and go talk to people. Get a friend who owes you a favor to help with the labeling so it gets done. Or label your own items and leave your spouse's unlabeled unless he does it. Keep the money from your things for yourself.

▶ **Even though I understand a lot more about ADD, my heart is burned out. Can I rekindle my love for my husband?**

Unfortunately that's a little hard to tell. In my years of counseling, I've seen fairly cool ashes rekindled. I've also seen people who chose to go their separate ways and were glad they did so.

You need to get rather philosophical about this. If it's meant to be, it will be. In the meantime, don't try to force anything. Pressure is the kiss of death. Look for little things to enjoy in each other and see what happens. Be open to feel the sweetness of love. It can happen.

▶ **My wife left me because of my irresponsibility. Now, I believe I have ADD. Our marriage never had a chance. How do I get over feeling awful about what happened?**

Attend to the grieving over the loss. Then find out all you can about ADD. Be properly diagnosed, join a support group, and start a new life for yourself. Learn, from this day forward, to make the most of what you have at any given moment. And learn from your experience so you don't make the same mistakes again.

▶ **If I don't take care of things around the house, the bills will never get paid, the repairs won't be made, and grass won't get mowed. I don't want to be codependent, but I'm tired of doing it all myself. Help!**

Do what you *want* to do for yourself and then give yourself a break. Reward yourself. Do not do for the person who is not holding up his or her share of the work load. If that person's un-picked-up clothing litters your living space and causes you to feel pain, ask him to pick it up and if he doesn't, either do it for yourself or pay to have it done and send him the bill. (Don't forget those to-do lists.)

114

Sadly, it is quite possible to love someone but not find them to be a compatible roommate. Set your priorities in order and make sure you get what you need most out of the relationship.

▶ **Why don't people with ADD like surprises?**

Surprises are intrusive. Sensitive people are going to feel the intrusion in extra measure. They also interrupt the steady flow of regularity. Remember people with ADD feel better and do better when they can count on what is going to happen.

▶ **If there's an emergency, what is the best way to get a person with ADD to react FAST?**

Act as calmly as you can. In a very matter-of-fact way, convey the information about the emergency directly to the person from close range in a moderate to low voice. Try not to yell across the room. Measure your words, telling the person what you need for him to do. Giving direction is much more helpful than simply stating that there is a crisis. Most people with ADD also like to know why they are being asked to do something. "I need you to immediately leave the house because it is on fire. If you will close the closet door, I will shut off the kitchen door and meet you outside."

◄ ◄ ◄ 11 ►► ►

For Intimate Couples

▼

*A*chieving and maintaining an intimate relationship, both emotionally and physically, can be quite a challenge for both the ADD person and the significant other. But, with an understanding of the ground rules—what works and what doesn't—the return on the effort is highly rewarding.

◄ What Not to Do

It's very easy in an ADD relationship to form codependent behavior. Simply put, the individuals focus their attention on each other rather than taking responsibility for themselves. In this scenario, an ADD person is likely to blame everyone or everything around for his problems, and the ADD person's significant other is likely to take responsibility for all the problems and for the necessary corrections.

"If only I'd remembered to remind her to make the bank deposit, her checks wouldn't have bounced," might be a typical line. Any time you hear a question like, "What can *I* do to get her to be more responsible?" it's a sure sign of enabling behavior. And, the person with ADD may blame the other person, too, demanding, "Why didn't you remind me?"

In such an unhealthy relationship, the partner of an ADD person often carries the role of the "responsible" one, the fixer who parents everyone. Growing up he or she may have been the one who could quiet Daddy down when he drank too much. Or maybe that person held Mommy's hand during a thunderstorm when Mommy was thirty-seven and the child was three. Fixers need to be needed, usually are controlling, and run things in an organized manner. But things had better be done their way—or else. It takes a lot of courage to let an ADD person mind his own business while the fixer finds other ways to feel valuable and lovable.

Usually it's easier to fix and complain and baby the ADD person.

Such mutual dependency tends to keep couples stuck—and I mean stuck—together, each attracted to the other because of feelings of inadequacy. Usually, too, people stuck in such a relationship are disappointed in each other because someone else can't fix their lives for them.

◀ Good Things to Do

But there are ways to avoid codependency and still be supportive of your ADD partner and of yourself, behaviors that you can use immediately to see improvement.

It's difficult to overestimate the value of one technique: If you live with an ADD person, ask him—or her—questions. It helps them process information. The questioning has to be done pointedly, but very gently, in a nonaccusatory way. The technique works especially well when the ADD partner is flooded, overwhelmed by the booming, buzzing world. "I've had it happen so many times when I'm flooded with information. I'm thinking of so many options that I can't do anything except yell or stomp off or shut down," says an ADD person. "When this happens, what usually works is for my mate to say, 'What are you feeling right now? Tell me what you're thinking and we can go through the options one by one.' This kind of approach helps me focus on what I really want to do instead of being bombarded by a thousand other things."

118

There's something that the ADD partner can do to help take the frustration out of the relationship: Take the initiative in dealing constructively with the "hardness" of tasks. How do you tell your loved one when something is too hard for you because of your ADD? The best way is—be blunt and ask for understanding from your mate. "This is too hard for me because of my ADD," is a positive way to put it. It's not an admission of weakness, but, rather, of special needs. And it could apply to no more than reading a map or picking from one of several spots to view wildflowers. At times when the ADD partner is overwhelmed, it's very helpful for the mate to say "Is there anything I can do to help you? What if we took it a piece at a time?" Or, "Do you just need to let the task go for now?"

Sound like codependence? Maybe, but it's not, and it's important for both of you to understand this. As the ADD person, you're asking for help, and in so doing, you're looking after your needs, a very healthy action to take. As the partner of the person with ADD, you don't do any part of the task for the ADD adult that he can do for himself. Neither do you take responsibility without being asked.

The result of these efforts will be a new-found emotional intimacy where both partners feel safe, appreciated, and accepted. You'll be able to share fears and secrets and tell each other intimate and personal thoughts—and each of you will be able to ask for help without feeling vulnerable or codependent.

Married women with ADD are at a special disadvantage in this society. Traditionally, women handle a lot of the detail work in the running of a household—running the kids to and fro, planning the meals, coordinating timetables and the thousand little details that make up daily life—but this is precisely the area where ADD people need the most help. Imposing responsibility for these details, without help or the knowledge that ADD is present, can create a frustrating and hopeless situation for the woman in the family. What appears to be a simple and easily managed average day can be a nightmare for these women. If they can't ask their mate for help, who can they ask?

◀ Touching

We've talked before about touching and the special problems—and pleasures—it can present for a person with ADD. Frequently, they don't want to be touched at all; it causes them pain. But, how do you tell someone close that you can't handle being touched right now, without hurting his or her feelings? When the partner needs or wants the contact, what can the person with ADD do that won't upset his partner but instead will convey a feeling of caring? One option to start with is the direct approach followed by saying what you can manage: "I'm feeling too sensitive right now. Could I just hold your hand or give you a quick hug, or just sit next to you?"

One woman wouldn't hug a man who had no awareness of his own strength. He'd always hurt her, even though she had told him many times that he was hurting her. His hugging felt painful to her. He just couldn't appreciate her sensitivity. So, she ducked his hugs and smiled a lot. Through small nuances and non-verbal communication, an ADD person often senses the ulterior motives of the person doing the hugging. The most common is a hidden sexual agenda. Generally, this kind of covert behavior breeds rejection, for she won't want to be touched by him.

Rhythmic touching, such as repetitive stroking or patting, usually annoys an ADD person. In its place, try gently and firmly grabbing an arm or a toe or one finger instead of a whole hand.

Although massages—the full-body type—may help reduce tension in many of us, they may be just too much of a good thing to an ADD person. If you and your ADD mate want to try massage as a pleasure-giving intimacy, try using oils to create a non-irritating touch, and keep the massage shorter, maybe to 30 minutes or so.

Experiment with variations. Once something pleasant is discovered, there is a strong possibility that the ADD person will not want to stick with it for very long. They in turn may find it difficult to believe the non-ADD partner likes the same thing repeatedly. Partners of ADD persons often find this phenomenon frustrating and have trouble getting the ADD person to repeat pleasurable touching.

Other Tips: Try hugging from behind instead of from the front. Or try putting the head of the ADD person in your lap. But be careful when you put your arm over the shoulder of an ADD person, especially a woman. The weight may feel too heavy.

◀ What About Sex?

Sex—so individual that it's difficult to generalize about it without making people uncomfortable, without leaving someone out, without violating someone's right to be different. Nevertheless, with ADD people, there are some generalities we can outline. The big generality is, simply, sex with (and for) an ADD person requires some understanding, or it's destined to cause frustration and dissatisfaction. This means that the ability to communicate verbally is essential to let personal needs and wants be known.

As importantly, from foreplay to location, variety is the key to sex with an ADD person. Remember, ADD people tend to get easily bored with the same thing. Fortunately, at least for them, they usually also have a willingness to experiment, to have sex in different ways in different settings.

An ADD person can get a lot out of foreplay if the individuals are comfortable with sex at all and if they mutually like each other and want each other. Because of the tension-relieving nature of sex, foreplay often acts as a reminder of pleasures to come. And usually, they don't have trouble concentrating on it, providing you keep it varied, and it's not prolonged. This is true even when the relationship is full of fighting and conflict. Sex makes them feel that they have some control: "Here's a person I care about, and I have a guaranteed outcome."

If the couple is not in tune with one another, loving and liking each other, the guaranteed outcome will not be there. A person with ADD can then be rejecting, feeling intruded upon by the partner's sexual desires or blaming the partner for the problems they are having. It's important that the partner accept no more than half the responsibility for the lack of fulfillment.

But, even with loving, caring couples, it's important to remember the ADD person's extreme sensitivity to pleasure and pain and the way they feel things strongly, and act accordingly. This characteristic can be used to advantage, if you do it right, and can lead to the greatest pleasure two people can share.

Some practical tips: One ADD person I know likes the light touch of fingernails drawn across her skin, but not too much in one place. Another likes being stroked with an ice cube, and another likes being licked (try honey or chocolate)—but, again never too long in one place.

Variation in sexual position follows the same rule of thumb: anything goes that will keep interest heightened. (Obviously the variation must be acceptable to both partners or not pursued at the expense of one.) Oral sex can fill the need for diversity but it is imperative that good hygiene be followed. Remember, all of the senses of a person with ADD are heightened. If his or her sense of smell or taste is offended, the desire for intimacy is squelched.

Because of the ADD person's sensitivity to pain, men must be especially mindful of finding comfortable positions for intercourse with an ADD female. Good communication and willingness to be flexible are essential here. ADD persons of either sex will experience the pressure of weight on top of them as more uncomfortable than most folks, so they may resist having the partner on top during intercourse. The key is understanding and the willingness to find positions that feel good to both participants.

Vary the location and environment for sex. Don't just have it in the bedroom, but try the living room or back seat of the car.

Try it in the swimming pool. Try turning off the air conditioner to build up a sweat. Switch from cotton sheets to satin sheets in the summer and flannel sheets in the winter. Remember, variety is the key for most ADD adults.

◀ Sexual Repression

There are exceptions, however, to this rule. After all, comfort with experimentation depends on how a person was trained about sex, whether they were raised with a sense of safety about it. Without such an upbringing, an ADD person may want no variability. Experimentation and prolonged sexual expression may seem too dangerous. Having sex the same way all the time may make him—or her—feel safe. Otherwise, he or she will make every effort to avoid sex—and exhibit the rigidity that some associate with Attention Deficit Disorder. There will be a tendency to make sex mechanical.

◀ When You're the Significant Other

Sounds like I'm talking about sex as a one-way street? Everything you can do for your ADD mate, sure, but what about you? It doesn't hurt to satisfy your mate's special needs, but what about yours? As with any intimate relationship without ADD, it's imperative that both participants are satisfied: no losers. Communication and consensus are the keys to making this happen.

There's nothing wrong with saying, "It's my turn now." One day, do it his way, the next, try it yours. Let your partner know what you like and ask. Don't demand, whine, or scold. Remember, most ADD people like humor, so it may do you well to add some instead of taking the sex game too seriously. Teasingly, you might say, "Watch out! I'll get you when you're least expecting it . . . . okay, not really. But let's play, huh?" It will be the lighthearted tone in your voice that will entice your lover.

Remember, the vulnerable feelings of an ADD person are soothed by reassurances that you won't hurt her. Better you learn to back off for a while than ruin the whole thing by impatiently trying to force sex. Say, "I'll stop if you want me to, but will you bring me to climax?" It's important that the ADD person not leave you hanging, so communicate your needs.

Consensus is a couple's best friend, not compromise. In the latter, neither gets what he wants. In consensus, together you find an alternative that pleases both. Don't give in and set yourself up as a loser. Don't get impatient because you are having trouble finding the solution. Say, "I know we'll find what is good for both of us. I love you."

If your partner will not work with you, you may need to be very clear that you can't do it all yourself. Sex is one area in which you cannot succeed alone, nor is it advisable to go outside the relationship for your satisfaction. It's better to face the fact that there is an unwillingness to work with you on sexual issues and get on with your life. Seek marriage counseling and be willing to call it quits if the willingness to try has vanished.

It is important to distinguish between a willingness to try and an ability to succeed. If you hear "I'm sorry," then you at least know you are being considered. You can be expected to be told you are important and lovable, which means your partner is taking responsibility for his part in this. ADD or not, no partner gets a free ride. Understanding, yes. A free ride, no.

◀ Common Questions About Intimacy

> ▶ **My wife has trouble maintaining eye contact in a conversation with me, keeps fiddling with things, and gets up and moves around instead of paying attention to me. Is she bored with me or could it be caused by ADD?**

It could be ADD and it might not be. A good diagnostic workup is essential to determine whether it is or not.

But, in an intimate relationship, ADD or not, you need to work at good communication. Ask your wife how she is feeling. Ask her whether it would be easier for her to talk with you in short segments.

Check to see what the style of your conversation is. Do you lecture, scold, go on and on, talk only about yourself, or monopolize the conversation?

▶ **I feel hurt because of her behavior. What can I do to feel better?**

Getting your feelings hurt is a great way to wreck a relationship. It puts responsibility for how you feel on the other person. Sounds like something you learned from your own past.

To remedy the situation, do two basic things:

◀ Look at your own expectations to see what it is you think your wife ought to be doing for you. Then do it yourself.

◀ Ask your wife whether she intended to hurt you with her behavior. She'll probably look utterly amazed and say, "No."

▶ **What can I do to make the situation better?**

Ask your wife to join you at a specific time and place, on a regular basis, so you can share some conversation and caring. Sometimes do what she suggests and sometimes you take the lead. A good marriage, with or without ADD, takes time and attention but the labor is worth it. Don't hesitate to work with a marriage counselor, if things don't get a lot better.

▶ **My husband, who has ADD, might be called the one-minute lover. I'm not making fun of him; it's just true. He has no need for foreplay, especially anything I might need or prefer. I need more—more intimacy, more of everything. What can I do?**

Find a neutral time, not when you are already in bed, to talk about the situation. Start with something positive like how much you care about him and would like making love with him.

Determine whether he has gotten into a bad habit of being thoughtless about you or whether he is truly suffering from a condition called premature ejaculation. A marriage counselor or sex therapist can help you with the latter. You and he can do a lot about the thoughtlessness.

Then, ask for his help. Take small steps, asking for a little fondling at first. Tell him how important it is to you. Be careful not to blame, criticize, or scold him about his lovemaking. But do make your point that you are important and want to have fun too.

Do not necessarily expect to climax at the same time. If he has already come, ask him to continue to make love to you until you do. Or turn it around and ask him to make love to you first.

Above all, do not make the remediation of the problem too serious. Add some fun along with a full measure of sensitivity and enjoy one another.

▶ **My partner wants to talk, and talk, and talk about sex: what she prefers, what made her feel good last night, and what she wants to try next. Is this because of her ADD? Just how much conversation about sex is necessary because of ADD and how much is due to other factors? Frankly, I find most of it boring.**

Although excessive talking is sometimes a symptom of ADD, there would be no particular reason for it to show up during lovemaking because of ADD. It could be nervousness or anxiety.

Some talk about your needs and hers seems indicated here if only for the sake of comfort. Do be sensitive, and for heaven's sake don't tell her you're bored. Make an "I statement," such as "I'm having trouble concentrating while you're talking. Would you tell me how the talking helps you? I'd really like to understand." Then listen.

She may be afraid because of past experience that her needs will be overlooked. Try to assure her that you want her to get what she wants and that you will work on it a little at a time. Be sure to ask her if she's pleased with whatever you do.

▶ **I'm a hugger, toucher, and feeler. It's just the way I am. I'm married to an ADD person who really doesn't like to be touched, at least not in the way I like to touch. What can we do? How can one of us not lose in this situation? Are we doomed for frustration or divorce?**

Since you are the one who likes to be touched, let her do the touching of you rather than vice versa. I wonder if you haven't been touching her as a way to initiate sex, which turns her off. Ask for what you want and you may have a deal.

127

The real trick in intimacy is to have no losers.
There is always a loser if force or coercion is
used. Therefore, you two must find ways to be
together that satisfy both of you. To accomplish
this, talk, experiment, and try some soothing
oils. Be sure with your ADD wife that you touch
her gently and firmly and don't stay in one place
very long. No tickling.

▶ **I have ADD, and it takes me a long time to
reach orgasm. I keep getting distracted, and
my partner eventually gets bored. What's the
solution?**

Taking a long time to reach orgasm is not likely
to be the result of ADD. Neither is your distractibility. First get a physical with your gyne-
cologist. Then, if all is okay, look for causative
factors in what you were taught about sex and
what your previous sexual experiences may have
been. If you were mistreated or were sexually
abused, you would have learned to distract
yourself as a psychological protection. It's hard
to turn your awareness back on, even though it's
now safe. Counseling offers a lot of good help
for this kind of problem.

▶ **When I sleep, I like to be tucked under the
covers and hold my wife like a pillow. She
hates it and says it feels like she's being suffo-
cated. Yet I have a hard time falling asleep
without it. What can I do?**

Better get yourself a real pillow to hug.

Occasionally embracing your wife would probably feel good to her. But using her like a pillow
for comfort is asking too much of her. Slowly
wean yourself away from the habit.

▶ **My wife, who has ADD, is really adamant when she talks about what she likes sexually. Yet it seems that what she likes changes constantly. I get confused. What does she *really* like?**

Variation.

▶ **If I suggest sexual experimentation, my husband, who has ADD, objects. But if he suggests it, then it's okay. Is this because he has ADD, or is he just a pig?**

One of the characteristics of people with ADD is a desire to be in control of things that affect them. Is it any wonder, since their own neurology put them out of control? But you count too. So, tell him you understand his need but you want to cut a deal, share and share alike. Mentally healthy people with ADD are very willing to share. If he is not, then it's not the ADD that is making him controlling; it's an emotional problem and you need to be firm that he really can't have only his way.

◄◄◄ **12** ►►►

When You Work with an ADD Person

▼

*H*aving become familiar with Attention Deficit Disorder, it is quite possible that you now see signs of it in people with whom you work. Or, worse yet, you think your boss demonstrates characteristics of ADD. But you can't go up to a co-worker or your boss and say, "I think you have ADD."

Sure, when you came for the job interview and met your new co-workers, there were no signs. But day in and day out, working with someone with untreated ADD has led to frustration, lost motivation, and feelings of resentment over having to do more than your fair share. And the worst part is that, unlike at home where you can blow off steam with your spouse, child, or parent, on the job you have to deal with the problem and your feelings about it without openly acknowledging that they even exist. *You* have to take responsibility for managing their ADD.

The following common questions and their answers will help you learn what you can do to make life easier on the job when you work with or for someone who has ADD but is not taking responsibility for it. These examples are taken from real life situations with real people who have either been diagnosed to have ADD or who believe they are working with someone with undiagnosed ADD.

131

▶ **My boss agrees to my plans one day and the next day tells me he never said "yes." How can he not remember what he said?**

Typical of ADD is a phenomenon in which the person says "yes" automatically, trying to be the good guy. Actually, when the "yes" is spoken, it may not be attached to a request in his mind. So, unbeknownst to you, your question never really got through.

▶ **My co-worker has all sorts of ideas but doesn't follow through on any of them. Is she just irresponsible?**

Could be. Might not be. Could be that her intent is to follow through but she gets distracted. She could be trying to be a good guy also, agreeing to develop much more than she can handle and getting lost in the aftermath.

To be honest with you, most people appear irresponsible but are trying the best they can. There could be other learning disabilities or emotional problems that are getting in the way of the completion of their objectives.

To protect yourself, don't depend on her for something you need done. Listen to her ideas but don't spend time putting work into them until she gets her ability to complete things under control.

▶ **My boss jumps from one topic to the next without resolving any of them. Business meetings seem pointless, but I can't refuse to attend. What can I do?**

◀ You can take a pad and do your own work during the meeting.

132

◀ From time to time you can suggest to your boss that you skip a meeting to complete a project.

◀ You can ask pointed questions during the meeting so that you get what you need out of it.

◀ You can listen to the topics your boss raises during the meeting, identify the ones that pertain directly to you, and, after the meeting, go to the people from whom you need input and get it personally rather than in the group. If you need further input from your boss, you might try getting it in writing.

▶ **Whenever I have something long or complicated to explain to my boss, he doesn't seem to be able to focus on what I'm saying. How can I communicate with him more effectively?**

Try putting what you have to say in written form. Maybe even outline it. Give him direct written questions to answer, preferably with "yes" or "no" answers.

If you talk with him, give him one question at a time. Get the answer to that one before going on to the next question. Don't expect to have lengthy conversations. Rather, touch base with him several times during the day so that your encounters are in small segments.

▶ **A co-worker doesn't keep her commitments, and I'm beginning to feel I can't trust her. But she is so likeable, and I don't want to just give up on her. What can I do?**

Separate your work needs from your personal feelings. You can enjoy her as a person even though you do not depend on her. For heaven's

133

sake, don't expect her to come through. She apparently isn't able at this time. So, if you expect follow-through on commitments, you're only setting yourself up for disappointment.

Also, give her permission to tell you "no" when you do ask her to do something. She may be succumbing to the good guy syndrome.

▶ **My boss can't seem to remember a production schedule he has worked with for years. Is he just not trying?**

It's possible he doesn't care and isn't trying but not likely. After all, it is his living also that's in jeopardy.

Unless he has a chemical abuse problem, he probably simply does not think about schedules, especially if he is a creative type of person. He may also get distracted by all sorts of issues that emerge in the daily running of a business or by his own ideas.

Your best bet to remedy the problem is to post a clear schedule, bring his attention to it regularly, and take as much personal responsibility as you can manage to keep up with it. Use his skills where they do shine. Some people just plain don't do well with schedules.

▶ **My boss is rigid and gets very upset if I deviate one little bit from the schedule he insists we use.**

Here's the flip side of the above coin. This boss has compensated for his deficits by rigidly adhering to a schedule. The reason is that, if he gets off of it a little bit, he'll get off of it a lot.

There tends to be no middle ground with people who have ADD.

▶ **The guy I work with just seems to bounce around. He has so much energy that he's like a puppy. How can I calm him down?**

There may be very little that you can do to calm him down. Though all people who have Attention Deficit Disorder have increased motor activity, only some have hyperactivity that is as noticeable as your coworker's.

The best you can do is to talk and move smoothly and soothingly. Your manner can calm him down a little. You may be able to affect him if you simply talk in a slower, soothing manner. Lower your voice. Try it.

▶ **Everyone likes our P.R. (public relations) director because she's so friendly and cheerful. But she just doesn't do well at her work. She's always distracted. I'm the one who has to follow through for her, but if I criticize her, I'm viewed as the bad guy. Is there any way to win in this situation?**

Be very straightforward with her, first of all. She needs to do something about her lack of follow-through. Tell her you have a problem because she doesn't produce on time, and tell her what you're going to do about it. Say, "I got into a real bind yesterday because your material wasn't ready. I know you're doing the best you can, and I like you a lot, but I can't run short again next week. Is there anything I can do to help you?" Don't set yourself up as a judge or criticize her.

If there continues to be a problem, ask her to join you for a discussion with your boss to work out a solution. That way you don't have to be the bad guy and you can get what you need.

If you are empathic with her, you may be amazed at how she may confide her fears and problems to you, considering you her good friend.

▶ **I hired a woman I thought was wonderful but she can't ever finish what she starts. My co-workers expect me to handle the work—she's my employee, after all. But if I criticize her work at all, she says I'm picking on her. What can I say to make things better? What are my options?**

How you bring her attention to inadequacies is important. If you tell her what's wrong without telling her how to fix it, she will feel helpless. After all, if she could have done it right in the first place, she would have. Instead, point out what you like or find acceptable in her work. Do this in a matter-of-fact way. Then show her how to apply that to something else she is doing.

Be sure to give her small assignments that are very specific. You may be giving her too much at one time so she can't focus. Give her breaking points in the work so she can naturally change her focus of attention rather than having it happen to her. What I'm talking about is providing more structure. (The armed services do it effectively. Take note.)

If your employee has an attitude problem, you can mention it to her, asking whether something is bothering her personally that she has been unable to leave at home.

Then, remember, if you hired her, you can fire her. You can do it humanely by taking responsibility. Say, "I made a mistake and hired you to do something that doesn't fit your capabilities. The job is not getting done, and you aren't getting the satisfaction of doing a job well." You may want to counsel her with regard to a job that would better suit her. You may also want to mention to her that you feel she may have an attentional problem that could be helped. Tell her you believe she is doing the best she can do and must be frustrated, but that help is available. Then refer her on to a counselor or support group that works with ADD *and* emotional problems.

If she still insists you are picking on her, say, "I'm sorry you feel that way, but it seems I can't do anything to change your mind." Then back off.

▶ **The wife of one of my best employees is a saleswoman. He is often late to functions, saying, "My wife just can't get anywhere on time." What could be the problem? What can he do to correct it?**

There are many reasons people are late. ADD is one, but by no means the only one. It could be her way of asserting her power in the relationship. (He wants her to be on time, so she gets to him by not being on time.) It could be an expression of the fact that she doesn't want to go.

What he can do to correct it is to take responsibility for getting himself to the function on time. He can come ahead and she can join him later. How he works that out with her is his business. You just keep the limit in place that you expect him on time and don't let him use his wife as an excuse.

137

▶ **My boss changes his mind about our plans all the time. He seems to jump from one idea to another. It causes me to make a lot of false starts, wastes a lot of my time, and makes me feel frustrated. How should I talk with him about this, and will it do any good?**

Go to him and say you appreciate the many ideas he has. Say, "But, I'm the kind of person who needs to follow through on ideas, and that's why you hired me. I need you to choose which idea you want me to work on to completion." Say it in a firm, slightly serious but warm manner. This lets him know you mean business but are not being critical.

When he again starts spewing off new ideas, make a list of them, taking the list to him along with a list of the projects you are already involved with. Ask him to set priorities. Say, warmly and firmly, "Remember, I need to feel good about finishing something." That way the burden is placed on him with regard to how you spend your time.

Most creative people, with or without ADD, appreciate having someone like you around. Your boss needs you desperately but just doesn't know how to use you. Help him learn.

If he is unwilling to work with you or fails to be nice about it, then look for another job.

▶ **One week my boss is incredibly excited about a project, demanding I act on it right away; the next week she's forgotten about it. Should I just ignore her fits of enthusiasm in the first place? Do you suppose I might be fired if I do?**

Gently point out a specific situation to her saying, "I was in the middle of Project A when you

138

asked me to start work on Project B, which you were very excited about at the time. Now, you have dismissed Project B. I'm confused. I need your help. I need to stick to one project until it is done or, if we switch gears, stay switched. What do you want me to do?

You will be talking to the reasoning part of your boss, not the emotional part (from which the new ideas come) and are likely to get a good, straightforward response as long as you don't sound critical.

Then ask her what she wants you to do if she again enthusiastically comes to you with a new idea. In her rational,reasoning mode, she will tell you what she needs. Then do it, and don't worry about getting fired.

▶ **I feel like I'm working with a toddler some-times. My co-worker has the shortest attention span I've ever seen. She'll stop talking in the middle of her own sentences or walk away in the middle of mine. What's the matter with her, and what can I do?**

She certainly has a rampant attentional problem. It could be caused by any number of things including emotional problems, ADD, a seizure disorder, or some other organic problem. Don't expect to diagnose it yourself.

What you can do is:

◀ Not take it personally.

◀ Keep your own conversations with her short.

◀ If she still walks away, go to her and ask whether she had a problem with what you were saying so you get some clarification for yourself.

139

◀   Accept her as she is and don't expect more than what she can give.

▶ **My boss only seems to want to dream and make big plans. I'm beginning to think he does this because of the excitement he gets out of it. Could that be?**

Sure could. There is a high (an adrenaline rush) that comes from the making of big plans. Some people get it from just having a wonderful idea. The feeling that comes from the high is so good that the person tends to want to feel it again and again. Once the feeling has passed, there is little interest in continuing to develop the plan. After all, it's pretty hard to get a rush from following up on mundane details.

▶ **Is there any future for me in a job where there's no follow-through by my boss on his dreams? What can I do to change things?**

Being in a dependent position in relation to a dreamer is risky unless that person is enough in touch with reality to appreciate what you bring to the situation. Dreamers need clear-minded thinkers and doers who can take responsibility to manifest their dreams. Your future depends upon your boss appreciating what you have to offer *and* giving you the power to do your job. That includes allowing you to set limits on him, such as saying, "No, we're not going to act on your new dream until we have completed work on the current dream project."

▶ **My boss comes into my office and demands I clean up my desk. He says no one could possibly do a good job with so much confusion. I know exactly where everything is and**

**can find what I need when I need it—and
quickly. Why can't he leave my desk alone?**

Your boss is assuming that because he is bothered by clutter on his desk, that you would be
too. Empathize with him, saying, "I realize the
shape my desk is in would make you feel confused, but my mind works differently and I do
better this way." Then reassure him, saying, "I'll
take responsibility to get my work done. Feel
free to criticize me on those grounds but leave
my desk alone." It won't hurt to add a bit of
humor to these statements.

If he comes in again and says something, jok-
ingly say, "Out of here."

▶ **Why would someone not do any of the things
necessary to get a big bonus based on the
completion of jobs when he is immensely
talented and seems to like what he is doing?**

It all depends on what those things are that he
has to do to get the bonus. His talent may simply
lie in other areas and he may prefer not to do
them. Money is not the primary reward for
many creative people. The chance to do what
they like to do may be more important.

▶ **My office mate can't seem to remember the
promises he makes me. Then he acts like a
little kid who should just be excused every
time. Does he just do that to play me along,
never intending to keep his promises in the
first place? What's his problem?**

First of all, your office mate probably learned
early in life that more was expected of him than
he could manage to do (not uncommon with

141

people with ADD). He also learned that if he promised he'd do something, his parents or teachers went easier on him. Such promises bought him time to try to figure out some way to please these important people. You see, all children desperately want to please the adults around them.

Unfortunately, no one realized that more was being expected than the little child could produce (also a common factor in ADD because the ability to produce results lags behind the general intelligence and capability of the child).

Then, to add insult to injury, your office mate was taught to say, "I'm sorry," whether he was really sorry or not. Unfortunately, this is common in our culture. It is the way he learned to get people off his back when he failed to follow through on something.

Your job is to tell him that you are more interested in his only committing to do what he knows he is willing to do, that you will like him even if he says "no" to you, and that you are more interested in problem solving when something isn't completed than hearing, "I'm sorry." Say, "Let's see what the problem is and figure out how to solve it. I know you care."

▶ **My boss just doesn't listen to me, because I'm telling him things he doesn't want to hear. But I'm the office bookkeeper and most of what I have to tell him isn't good news. What can I do?**

    ◀ Keep your sense of humor.

    ◀ Realize that he is running away from things that cause him anxiety.

◀ Rather than telling him the problem first, which raises his anxiety level, tell him something he can do to fix the problem.

◀ A lot depends on how close he will let you get to his feelings. If your relationship warrants it, you can get right up in his face and talk turkey to him, confronting him. But you have to have someone's trust to do that.

◀ Realize the limits of your power. You are the employee and he's the boss. If he continues to run, he's committing business suicide and you cannot take the responsibility to stop him. You can only try to help him.

◀ Be protective of yourself if you realize the company may be going under, and start looking for other opportunities.

▶ **Our sales manager can't seem to organize his own time. I see this in other sales reps also, so I'm not sure I'll do much better if I fire him. Besides, he makes good sales. Any suggestions?**

There is a higher than average number of people with ADD who are drawn to sales positions, often doing very well. However, organization is often not their strong suit (though some have mastered the problem by being *very* organized).

Keep paper work to a minimum. Try providing simple, clearly structured report sheets. Have the person take part in the development of the reporting form. As you see from the samples in Chapter 9, different people with ADD handle their structuring differently. Be flexible.

If no choice is available, break the task into small segments, so, rather than doing all the

reports on Friday, have him do them daily.
(Don't be surprised, though, to discover that
when he is on the road, he'll avoid doing the
reports until the last minute. Many of us tend to
have an aversion to doing what we don't like, so
we put it off.)

Empathize with your errant salesperson and be
grateful for what you do have.

Consider hiring a clerk so the salesperson only
has to collect raw data that someone else puts in
boxes. Then, the salesperson can go out and sell
more to pay for the clerk.

▶ **My business partner never does what he says
he is going to do. But if I get irritated with
him, he just falls apart. Why is he like this?**

He probably has a long history of people getting
mad at him for not producing what he is supposed to produce. And, if he's a typical ADD
person, he has a great need (who among us
doesn't) to be liked. So he falls apart because
he feels awful.

Now, I'm going to pin you to the wall. Why do
you feel irritated? We can observe a problem
without getting emotionally upset, unless there
is something for us to learn from the situation
about ourselves. Many folks, however, tend to
put the responsibility for their feelings on others.

Ask yourself, "When else in my life have I been
in a situation in which someone has let me
down, saying they would do something and
then not following through?" You may remember when your dad said he'd go to your
ballgame to watch you play. You told all the kids
he was coming and he never showed up. PAIN!

144

Though your irritation may come from a less painful memory, there will be something for you to learn. His lack of follow-through may cause you to have to do more work or compromise your safety or security.

Knowing the cause of your irritation can help you remove it from your conversation with your partner. Then you can talk in matter-of-fact, non-critical business terms that will get to the real issues rather than emotional issues.

Lay out the tangible business needs you have, ask your partner to commit to only what he is willing *and* able to do. (Many people with ADD *want* to produce more than they are actually able to produce.)

Your partner must get beyond his part of this problem so you can count on him to be trustworthy. Otherwise, it is not wise to be in a partnership that can compromise your security.

On occasion, it may be worthwhile to stay in the partnership, working behind the scenes to do both your work and what your partner promises to do, *if* you are getting something else of value from him, such as financial backing. Just know the price you are paying for the backing and don't expect more.

▶ **I know my boss is intelligent, but sometimes he doesn't act like it. He can't seem to focus on giving me work to do in an efficient manner so I come off looking bad. What can I do to protect myself from looking bad?**

Don't expect your boss to do the organizing. You do it. No matter how intelligent your boss, you may be a much better organizer. Or work with him to get organized.

145

▶ **Another manager in our department has terrible work habits but keeps getting awards for innovative ideas. But she never follows through on them, and her paper work is a mess. I try very hard and have good work habits but get overlooked. Why does upper management notice her all the time? What can I do to get noticed?**

Apparently upper management hasn't caught on to the fact that she doesn't follow through. Patience, my dear. Sooner or later, they will realize the problem unless they value ideas without follow-through.

To get noticed, you may need to call their attention to a completed project. Blow your own horn. Were you by any chance taught that that was not the thing to do to be polite? Or worse yet, maybe it wasn't even safe for you in your family to be noticed. Work on these issues within yourself so you can show your stuff off.

Finally, you may, after some patience, decide that there is not a good fit between you and upper management. At·that point, get another job where you and your skills will be valued.

Epilogue

▼

*P*eople with ADD are drawn to me like bears to honey. I, in turn, love the wonderful characteristics that are part of some of the sweetest, most sensitive people in the world. I married a person with ADD, though I didn't realize it at the time. I reared one. My oldest son chose one to love. My personal friends are disproportionately weighted in that direction. The people I have connected with through radio, television, and public appearances frequently have had more than their fair share of ADD symptoms, and my private practice has brought me in touch with many others with whom I have been able to work effectively.

I began to wonder one day why, or how, this magnetism between me and so many ADD persons had developed. The answer, I believe, lies in characteristics we share—and in ones we don't.

I am very sensitive, and feel things deeply. I am creative by nature and in my approach to problems. I am learning disabled (though not because of ADD), so I know the feeling of lost potential first hand. I'm empathic with regard to the feelings of others. All these traits I share with people who have ADD.

But I am different from them in several important ways. I can stay focused on a task for a very long time. I am patient and soothing, and become more so when I am around someone who is scattered, stressed, or out of control. Such differences complement my ADD friends and relatives.

I truly admire the characteristics displayed by people with ADD. I also feel the pain they have felt. Communicating this understanding builds an instant bond between us. I also have skills to help them heal this pain and grow beyond the difficulties they encounter. A more grateful group of people I have never met.

People with ADD tend to wear their emotions on their sleeves. Holding few secrets, they display their feelings and thoughts to the world. They know what it's like to be hurt, and because they crave acceptance and understanding they often readily accord it to others. They are easier for me to deal with than people who do things because they should, rather than from the depths of their hearts. I would rather know right out front what I'm dealing with than play games of pretense and secrecy.

In my dealings with ADD, I've also learned to look at it in another way—to look at what I'm tempted to call its advantages. It's difficult to fool people with ADD. They look past surface appearances and facades to the core of people and issues and evaluate them with down-to-earth standards. They tend to be good networkers because they see so many relationships between people and things.

Also, because they don't suffer from the boundary isolation that we "normal" people are afflicted with, they are able to put new projects together readily. They can cross disciplines or skill areas, drawing from what attracts their attention. Without the boundaries that confine non-ADD people, they focus on relationships found between the disciplines. Because they can so easily switch their attention from one thing to another, they do not get in a rut.

Their sometimes chaotic perception makes them originals, with a marvelous sense of humor, the stand-up comics of the world, flipping from one train of thought to another. They don't miss a cue. At the best of times, they are fun to go places with because they see things the rest of us don't see. They are observers par excellance. If you've lost something, call your nearest ADD friend. They are more likely to find it than the average guy. Their observatory power is why they make good sales people, broadcasters and journalists, and entrepreneurs.

The wealth of talent and goodness possessed by people with ADD tends to be ignored. Creative and spontaneous, these often-misunderstood folks may be one of the great unrecognized treasures of our land. They are a national resource that can be tapped. All it will take is understanding, some adjustments in the educational process to better fit their style of learning, and awareness on the part of parents so that they adjust their parenting styles. Children with ADD can be taught to adjust for their condition, speak out about it, and, as they mature, put themselves in learning and work environments that will use their talents and gifts effectively. ADD, really, is not much different from wearing glasses.

The disorder, for let's not forget that that's what it is, provides people with a different way of looking at the world and creates the need for a different way of learning. Trying to fit ADD people into the normal world order only causes problems for the system and the ADD person. They usually benefit from an opportunity to move around, do projects in short segments, and be creative in their approach to tasks. If an ADD person is told the desired outcome and allowed to develop his or her own way of arriving at that outcome, the project is more likely to succeed.

But try to squeeze an ADD person into a stereotypical pattern and there is likely to be a lot of hollering and wasted energy. So concentrate on the intent of the project or activity. Specify the desired outcome. This is critical when working with someone who has ADD.

Most importantly—throw the rule book aside! Let the ADD person develop his own path and his own timetable. If you

149

do this, you are likely to get an A-1 job out of the ADD person.

On the other hand, the loss of potential through underachievement, drug and alcohol abuse, and delinquent behavior caused by untreated ADD is a crime on its own. It costs taxpayers millions of dollars every year, wrecks the lives of innocent people, breaks up marriages, and carves a path of destruction and pain for the victims and their family members.

Yet those losses needn't occur. ADD can be diagnosed at an early age—or any time afterwards. Adults with ADD can turn their lives around. Through therapy they can right previous wrongs, breaking the cycle of devastation that is passed from generation to generation.

Though I'm not much of an activist or placard carrier, I am campaigning for awareness of this very treatable condition. Please join me for yourself, your loved ones, and your friends.

◀ A Few Last Questions About ADD

▶ What are the advantages to having ADD?

Advantages to having ADD include creativity, an ease in sharing their thoughts and feelings, and a tendency to offer acceptance and understanding to others. People with ADD have a high degree of sensitivity and empathy.

They do not tend to be "should" people but do what they feel. They can look through facades and see people and issues clearly. They do not have boundary isolation, i.e., they do not limit themselves to one area, but rather see the similarities between things. So they are good at interdisciplinary and cross-disciplinary skills. They are very intense when very interested in something.

▶ **Aren't there other ways to get these traits?**

Sure. Not only is not every person with ADD
necessarily creative, but not all creative people
have ADD. There are many reasons why each of
the traits develops in different people. It's just
that people with ADD tend to have them as a
kind of side effect of their condition.

▶ **What is boundary isolation?**

It is a kind of territoriality on a mental or emotional level. Our culture tends to be very territo-
rial. One profession doesn't want anyone
schooled outside of that profession to be able to
ply the skills identified as belonging to that profession. Labels are attached to the categories regardless of the similarities in the way they may
function.

In boundary diffusion, the opposite is true. Similarities in function are what is important. The
category in which the skill belongs is irrelevant.

For example, the best training I ever received
for counseling people came from my graduate
work in anthropology, where I learned a research method called "participant observation."
But rather than applying it to anthropology, I
became aware that it was exactly what happens
in counseling when the therapist affects the
client(s) by his or her very presence. So I applied
what I learned across disciplines. Then I applied
it to parenting, managing my office staff, etc.
And it doesn't matter to me that participant observation is generally considered to be a tool of
anthropologists; it is still useful.

This is what happens in boundary diffusion.

APPENDICES

An Open Letter to Potential ADD (Attention Deficit Disorder) Sufferers

▼

Attention Deficit Disorder is one of those conditions that often goes unrecognized as the culprit beneath other problems that plague a person in the growing years. It is not unusual in adolescence for people with ADD to self-medicate with drugs and alcohol, to do poorly in school even though bright. "You could do better if you'd just try," is a common complaint leveled at a sufferer, who comes to believe that, indeed, he or she ought to be able to pay attention and produce.

Active, creative, restless, explosive, requiring variability in all areas of life, the person with ADD can be channeled to find a place in adult life that fits. But all too often the criticisms and abuse of early years leave their mark on the self-confidence and self-esteem of the adult. The ADD adult *believes* himself/ herself to be of lesser stock or inferior quality than peers because of a condition that makes its mark in terms of the way the person experiences the world.

Diagnostic criterion for ADD include:

A history (often undiagnosed) of ADD must be present in childhood. (A hyper kid, he or she talked too much, bounced around the classroom, tended to get in more trouble than other kids for small things, and didn't seem to learn from experience because he or she continually did things over and over.

154

This kid didn't like school much and often was criticized and even abused because of problems concentrating, staying on task, and sitting still.)

Also there must be both attention and motor abnormalities in the adult. Typically, these show up in difficulty completing a task if not particularly interested in it. (A well socialized person will complete the task but inwardly will need to use an inordinate amount of effort to do so.) Often this criterion is used as a criticism, "You could do it if you wanted to." Those of us who do not have ADD can do it even if we don't want to, but an ADD person is much more likely to be distracted if he is not interested in the task at hand.

Difficulty in maintaining concentration in conversation with others, particularly in groups, is prevalent. Listening to verbal reports, lectures, and meetings is also hard for the ADD person.

The abnormal motor behavior takes two forms in adulthood. First, is motor restlessness. (Always on the go. An inability to relax unless fatigued. Once the person sits or lies down, they are likely to go to sleep or blob out, couch potato style, in front of the TV.) The restlessness may be subtle with shifting of the weight, lots of trips to the water cooler, and movement disguised as involvement in many activities. These forms are more apparent when a person has been well socialized and is trying very hard to do what is "right".

Fidgetiness is the second form of motor abnormality. This includes finger and toe tapping, sometimes disguised by the subtle depression of the appendage so that no one really notices. Leg swinging, seat shifting, and general continuous motion are apparent often.

In addition to the above two characteristics of ADD in adulthood, two of the following five traits need to be present: poor impulse control; mood abnormalities; short or excessive temper and or irritability; poor organization with poor task completion; and low stress tolerance with over-reactivity.

155

People with poor impulse control have difficulty in delaying gratification, are unable to anticipate consequences, and say things on the spur of the moment. They frequently act without thinking. I've often been told by ADD patients that "if I don't do something immediately, I'll never get it done because I'll get distracted." Breaking into a conversation, buying impulsively, drinking impulsively, and other similar behaviors often bring severe repercussions and certainly can disrupt social relationships.

Mood abnormalities include feeling very, very good and very, very bad, often within a short period of time. However, the mood changes are usually environmentally related. The person with ADD also gets over the downs quickly, especially if the outside situation rights itself.

Poor organization with an inability to complete tasks occurs as the ADD person jumps from one thing to another. Some ADD people have a good ability to structure their work but may still have problems in actually following the structure they themselves have created. It is not unusual for a person with ADD to live in a state of mental and physical clutter and it is important to not overload the person with too much new input too quickly.

Low stress tolerance and overreactivity looks like "emotional thin skin." Actually, when you consider the problems in screening out stimuli, the ADD person is reacting appropriately to their screening mechanism. Their screening mechanism is just a lot less effective than that of people without ADD. So, ADD people are easily flustered, feel hassled, tense, or uptight. They make mountains out of molehills and crises constantly disrupt their life.

People with ADD like vibration, rock and roll, drums, soothing partners, and freedom of motion. When the condition is understood and guilt over past and present inabilities to "control" oneself is let go, an ADD person can make adjustments that allow for a perfectly happy life in which his or her attributes are seen as assets rather than liabilities.

156

Diagnosis of ADD
in Adults

▼

◀ American Psychiatric Association
Diagnostic and Statistical Manual

The Diagnostic and Statistical Manual (DSM) published by the American Psychiatric Association contains definitions and codes for psychiatric conditions, including Attention Deficit Disorder. The information is used to communicate between physicians and other medical personnel, insurance companies, and anyone involved with the treatment of the person diagnosed to have a condition included in the book.

Often the definition impacts who is identified as having a condition and therefore who gets treated; how he is treated; and how much money the person will pay out-of-pocket for the treatment. Insurance companies, agencies, and programs (such as the rehabilitation commissions) of the various states will set their parameters for treatment based on what is included under the categories of the DSM.

In 1980, Attention Deficit Disorder in Adults made its debut in DSM-III. It was listed in the section on "Disorders Usually First Evident in Infancy, Childhood or Adolescence." The disorder was called Attention Deficit Disorder, Residual Type, and given a code of 314.80.

> *Diagnostic criteria for Attention Deficit Disorder,*
> *Residual Type*
>
> A. The individual once met the criteria for Attention Deficit Disorder with Hyperactivity.

157

This information may come from the individual or from others, such as family members.

B. Signs of hyperactivity are no longer present, but other signs of the illness have persisted to the present without periods of remission, as evidenced by signs of both attentional deficits and impulsivity (e.g., difficulty organizing work and completing tasks, difficulty concentrating, being easily distracted, making sudden decisions without thought of the consequences).

C. The symptoms of inattention and impulsivity result in some impairment in social or occupational functioning.

D. Not due to Schizophrenia, Affective Disorder, Severe or Profound Mental Retardation, or Schizotypal or Borderline Personality Disorders.

That category was dropped from the DSM-III-R published in 1987. Rather, an insert appeared that read:

314.00 *Undifferentiated Attention-deficit Disorder* This is a category for disturbances in which the predominant feature is the persistence of developmentally inappropriate and marked inattention that is not a symptom of another disorder, such as Mental Retardation or Attention-deficit Hyperactive Disorder, or of a disorganized and chaotic environment. Some of the disturbances that in DSM-III would have been categorized as Attention Deficit Disorder without Hyperactivity would be included in this category. Research is necessary to determine if this is a valid diagnostic category and, if so, how it should be defined.

The fourth addition of the *APA Diagnostic and Statistical Manual* is scheduled for publication in 1993. Considerable

158

discussion is underway by professionals and laypeople regarding the inclusion of a category for Attention Deficit Disorder in adults. Both the placement within the manual and
criteria to be included are being debated.

> Because of the power inherent in the diagnostic
> coding of conditions, it is important that legiti-
> mate conditions and syndromes be accurately
> reflected in the diagnostic manual. The history
> of this coding for ADD in adults is inconsistent
> in the manual and it has recently caused con-
> siderable concern, reflected in an article in
> *ADDendum*, Issue #5, Summer, 1991, p. 7.

For input into the committee overseeing DSM-IV Disruptive
Disorders Committee, write:

> DSM-IV Disruptive Disorders Committee
> c/o Nancy Sydnor-Greenberg
> American Psychiatric Association
> 1400 K Street, N.W.
> Washington, D.C. 20005

Following, I've included a letter that I chose to write as a
concerned citizen and professional.

Learning to Live with ADD: Five Stages

▼

While mingling with over three hundred participants at the first conference solely dedicated to serving adults who have ADD, the light bulb went off in my head. As it did, tears threatened to escape for all to see. I was viewing the happiness, healing, and growth of adults who previously had been lost or wanting, or whose lives were in disarray.

All around I recognized people with intense emotions; happiness, sadness, anger, excitement, euphoria, peacefulness were being expressed. These wonderful people were experiencing different levels of awareness and understanding about their ADD. I began to realize that what I was seeing were the stages through which people go as they integrate information about their ADD into their daily living. Five distinct stages emerged.

Stage One could be called the "Aha, I have it," stage. "Finally I have an explanation for why my life is the way it is. There really is *something* different about me. But I'm not crazy, retarded, lazy, or no good." This is a time of awakening. It's recognition that "there are others like me." "I'm not the only one." Shock, excitement, and euphoria are likely to accompany this time as well as an insatiable search for information.

Stage Two can be called the grief stage. Once the realization sinks in that there was a reason for not being able to live up to potential, the hurts, traumas, and losses suffered because of ADD begin to surface. As the mind begins to recall the hundreds of incidents that were related to ADD, the emotions begin to react. Confusion, anger, "what ifs," and depression

160

all churn, creating emotional bedlam. This stage does end, but first it is important to feel the emotions and grieve the losses in order to heal the wounds.

Stage Three involves seeking support and understanding companionship during the grieving stage. This stage could be called the family stage. Over and over at the Adult ADD Conference, I heard people say, "I've found my family. There are others like me. I plan to come every year to my family re-union." Not only can information and guidance be gained at such groupings, but all important emotional support can be obtained. "Coming home" to a place of unconditional accept-ance heals the wounds of the past and supports the growth of the future.

Stage Four is characterized by seeking, exploration, and ex-perimentation. It might be called the growing up phase. It's a time for trying things. With ADD factored into a person's life, suddenly everything looks different. Exposure to previ-ously tried experiences is necessary in order to discover from the new ADD perspective whether you like or dislike them, can or can't do them, want or don't want to pursue them now. It's an updating of data in one's bank of life experience.

Stage Five means coming of age. It is surely a time for the un-folding of a new identity. It's a time to redefine values, honor talents and gifts, and love who and what you are. "I know who I am now. I believe in myself. I can do whatever I've dis-covered I like. I am me." Reaching potential is wonderful, beautiful, and heady stuff. It is also possible and real.

The integration of current information into the life experi-ences of innumerable people is opening the door for the de-velopment of the most valuable resource known to mankind: individual identity. As differences are recognized and hon-ored, not only will individuals' lives be made more pleasant, but the world will truly become a better place in which to live. Let us provide support through the five stages of healing and growth of those with ADD in a context of understanding and acceptance. Then everyone wins.

Sample Adult ADD Assessment Interview

▼

A two-part interview has proven to be beneficial in the assessment of Attention Deficit Disorder in adults. The first session is an interview covering childhood and adult behavior. Complete school and family histories are taken; histories of personal life and job experiences as well as parental histories need to be extensive. In addition, an ADD checklist is completed by both the person suspected of having ADD and the interviewer.

It has been found to be very helpful to have a "significant other" (spouse, parent, friend, etc.) present for the assessment portion of the two interviews. Adults with ADD sometimes will not see their behavior as problematic or different, and having another person present can be very helpful.

It is good to get the ADD person to tell the complete story of what happened during any particular incident. They have so often been blamed for their lack of control that they assume they are at fault and do things for no good reason. When the details come out, especially in a supportive, non-judgmental setting, another picture of the incident may appear. I also always ask about the *intent* behind an ADD person's actions. That often has the effect of gaining their trust and produces a fuller picture.

PART I

◀ School History

Attempt to gather as much information about school experience as the client remembers, as far back as the client remembers. What was school like for them? (Fun, hassle, enjoyable, depressing, something to try to get out of?). Did the person get in trouble more than the average kid? Was there a lot of daydreaming? (Check to see if this was a label put on the child or whether the person intentionally sought to fantasize.) Was following what the teacher was doing easy, hard, etc.? (Was recess the best time of the day?) Did he "lose interest" in courses which in turn led to problems with them? Was the person the one who was always talking with others, a class clown, "picking" at others, having trouble staying seated? How involved were the parents in their school? (Up at school a lot at the request of the school? Prodding at home to get homework done? Making sure the child finished things?) If the person attended college, what major was chosen and why? What attention/concentration problems remained in college?

When ADD is present, symptoms persist throughout school. Many have much difficulty when they become adolescents. Key times that difficulties are likely to show up are 4th and 7th grades and at the beginning of high school. Each of these grades tends to present the person with a new level of complexity both cognitively and environmentally.

◀ Family History

In talking about family, I usually ask the person to tell me about his or her family, what it was like growing up, what relationships were like between him and his siblings and parents, how the parents got along with each other, and how the child fit into the lineup. Was there divorce, separation, family problems, fighting or violence, physical, verbal, or substance abuse, or other addictions (eating disorders, sexual addiction, workaholism, spending problems, etc.)? Was the person abused: verbally, psychologically, physically, (including being spanked a lot), or sexually?

Get the parent's history, in school, work, and parenting. Does one or both parents have a temper, short fuse, or spank first/ ask questions later behavior style? (Remember, many parents will turn out to have undiagnosed ADD too.)

◀ Personal Life

A brief personal history of the client focusing on the personal feelings, relationships, pleasurable activities and hobbies, goals and desires in life, and hopefulness for the future is necessary. Many times ADD adults will experience an overall feeling of depression and lack of personal fulfillment. Relationships may be volatile and/or the person may have trouble maintaining long-term ones. Intimacy can be difficult for persons with ADD.

People with ADD frequently need to relieve the stress that accumulates for them in daily living. TV, video games, music, racing (cars), and anything that has a vibration or hypnotic repetition, including jogging, are prime candidates for activities. Check for addictive behavior also, such as overspending, eating disorders, jogging addiction, chocoholism, or any behavior engaged in with a vengeance.

Another good personal question has to do with the use of free time. What favorite hobbies or activities are preferred? This tells you what makes the person comfortable, even the well socialized one, when he doesn't have to feel responsible to do what he *should* do. Often persons with ADD will engage in hobbies that do not require great attention for extended periods of time. Golfers with ADD make use of the high degree of structure required by the game. Thrill-producing activities like race car driving rate high, as does street basketball or cruising, which allows the person to change direction at will. Music, dancing, and performing to a beat are often associated with ADD.

◀ Physical History and Status

Take a current and past health history. Inquire about childhood ailments and physical habits with special attention to sleep and eating habits. Ask about chronic conditions of a mild as well as a debilitating nature. Ask whether the person has had falls. Pay particular attention to times when his or her head was involved, regardless of whether loss of consciousness occurred. Inquire whether the ADD-like symptoms began to occur after an illness or injury. (Then it's not ADD.) Should there be a question about other organic problems including infection, head injuries, or seizure disorders, brainmapping may be required to obtain a clear diagnosis.

Take a complete history of drug and alcohol use with the person as well as the parents and grandparents. Encourage the person to be forthright. Include questions about diet pills and the results the person experienced after the use of prescription or street drugs. (It's not uncommon for a person to get instantly "smarter" or more organized when taking diet pills. "Speed" and cocaine also can produce positive results for people with ADD. The side effects, however, preclude their use, as does their illegality. There seems to be a need for people with ADD to anesthetize their feelings. Alcohol, though ineffective in the long run, is often used to excess.

◀ Job and Career History

Take a complete job history. Inquire about the person's interest in the job, which aspects were easy and which were hard and what the person prefers. A large number of people with ADD go into sales, the entertainment business, and outdoor work such as landscaping. Inquire about reasons for leaving any jobs. Be supportive so that the person is not threatened by the

165

questions. Find out whether the person left voluntarily, was fired, or work ran out. Ask about the specific circumstances surrounding separation from the job. (Temper and organization problems are not unusual with people with ADD.) Look for job hopping and multiple job experiences. Ask about how the person got along with supervisors and what kinds of people the person liked to work for. Many people with ADD have problems with overbearing authority and critical types of management. They work best with positive, supportive reinforcement. Threats get nowhere and usually will cause an ADD person to bolt.

◀ Parent Interview

If parents are available, interview them with regard to the preschool years. Begin in infancy, especially with sleep, eating, and comforting patterns, response to noise, change, mobility habits, and physical conditions including colic, allergies, and irritability. Ask about parent involvement in school, calls to the school, teacher complaints, and involvement with homework. Check out accident proneness, breakage around the house, relationships with siblings, and disruptive interpersonal relations between the person and other family members and other kids. (People with ADD tend to have difficulty getting along with others because of impatience, temper problems, short attention spans, and a tendency to have difficulty waiting their turn. They also tend to mature behaviorally at a slower rate than others do.)

◀ Spouse or Friend Interview

Get the observations of a spouse or friend. Cover behavioral, interpersonal, emotional, and interest areas. Ask for vignettes. You might say, "What is it like to do yard work with this person?" or "What's it like to sleep with her?" or "Tell me the story of the last time you two went shopping, or did your income tax together."

◀ ADD Checklist 1

(Ask for specific examples) Adapted from DSM-III

	Yes	Some	No
Often fails to finish things started	____	____	____
Often does not seem to listen	____	____	____
Easily distracted	____	____	____
Has difficulty concentrating on sustained-attention tasks	____	____	____
Has difficulty sticking to an activity, especially one not desired	____	____	____
Often acts before thinking	____	____	____
Shifts excessively from one activity to another	____	____	____
Has difficulty organizing work or becomes disorganized if not following a schedule	____	____	____
Benefits from a structured environment	____	____	____
Frequently calls and talks out, interrupting conversations	____	____	____
Has difficulty waiting his turn in group situations	____	____	____
Impatient	____	____	____
Excessively on the move, often falling asleep when still	____	____	____

	Yes	Some	No
Has difficulty sitting still or fidgets excessively	——	——	——
Has difficulty staying seated	——	——	——
Moves about excessively during sleep	——	——	——
Always "on the go"	——	——	——
Engages in more than one activity at a time	——	——	——
Very sensitive to rejection, teasing, criticism, and frustration	——	——	——
Shifts moods suddenly and unexpectedly but based on events	——	——	——
Hot temper that disappears quickly (doesn't hold grudges)	——	——	——
Frequent negative thinking after excitement	——	——	——
Hard to give and take soothing and holding	——	——	——
Is soothed and/or aided in focusing by use of TV, radio, or fan	——	——	——
Tends to blame others	——	——	——
Stand-up comedy tendencies	——	——	——
Responds to asking better than being told	——	——	——

Yes responses to 40 percent of the above is indicative of ADD in adults when accompanied by a history of these behaviors in childhood.

◀ ADD Checklist 2

A checklist that I find very useful in diagnosing ADD was developed by Dr. Kathleen Nadeau ("ADHD in Adults—Diagnosis and Treatment," *HAAD Enough,* Nov/Dec 1990, p. 7).

Some signs of Attention Deficit Disorder in Adulthood Include:

1. Chronic forgetfulness

2. Problems with time management (problems estimating realistically how long a given task will take and then allotting that time to the task)

3. Tendency to take on far too many tasks or projects

4. Generally disorganized lifestyle—frequently late, rushed, unprepared

5. Difficulty managing check book and finances

6. Frequent moves and/or job changes

7. Tendency to speak without considering the reaction which may be elicited by their comment

8. Tendency to interrupt others in conversation

9. Difficulty controlling temper

10. Difficulty managing paperwork on the job

11. Chronic pattern of underachievement (i.e., bright, but didn't excel in school; less advanced in career than others with the same years of experience)

12. Pattern of establishing relationships with caretakers—maybe a spouse, roommate, or secretary who serves as memory and organizer

13. Pattern of periodic depression which may begin in adolescence

14. Difficulty in maintaining long-term relationships (may have multiple marriages)

15. Greater than average tendency toward substance abuse

16. Tendency toward impulsivity—may make major decisions such as car purchases, home purchases, or job changes without careful, long-term planning

17. Tendency to be either over-active or under-active, with a previous history of overactivity

18. Low tolerance for frustration—tendency to overreact to frustration

19. Tendency to give up on difficult, long-term projects

20. Pattern of interests which are taken up, then dropped, often after the investment of substantial sums of money in the pursuit of each interest

21. Difficulty concentrating when reading

22. Difficulty handling demanding learning situations which may be required for job advancement

23. Pattern of achieving less than siblings, academically or professionally

◄ Observation

The interviewer needs to make careful notes with regard to physical and attentional behavior during the interview. Watch for subtle as well as flagrant signs. Shifting of weight, finger drumming, and foot swinging are often present in excess. A need to get up and move around may be present. Accommodation of these behaviors does not interfere with the assessment and is the only kind thing to do for the person.

There is likely to be considerable sadness and even pain associated with some of the childhood and, at times, adult memories. Feelings of loss, shame, and inadequacy are quite common. Understanding and compassion are called for at these times. Sometimes, the person has bought into the system that accused and criticized him with how he "should" have been able to behave. It is common for an adult with ADD to put himself/herself down as a child, saying, "I just didn't listen" or "I just didn't try hard enough." This is a case of the victim joining the perpetrator. It is important to make it safe during the interview for the person to be able to be honest about actually having tried as hard as he or she could.

PART II

This session covers the results of the information gathered in Part I. It is preferable to allow at least three days between Parts I and II. Ask the person if he or she has had any other thoughts or feelings since the assessment. Clear up any questionable areas or concerns that you may have. Then, if you feel that the person has Attention Deficit Disorder, provide a skill building and remediation group, a study skills group if the person is in school, and a medication check if desired by the person. All referrals need to be prescreened to be sure the professional has experience with ADD. Unfortunately many professionals don't and will either discount the condition or give inappropriate support. Traditional psychotherapy is rarely indicated. Any work with interpersonal skill building, tutoring, or personal trauma reduction must take into account the special needs of the person with ADD. Traditional methods simply fall short.

A report and referral letter is indicated and it is recommended that these be shared with the person, who is seen as a partner in the evaluation and retraining process.

A three-month follow-up is indicated.

Sample Clinical Report Summary

▼

*A*fter you have determined by an assessment with a diagnostician that you have Attention Deficit Disorder, he or she will put together a report similar to the sample given here. With your permission, that report will be submitted to your therapist, doctor, employer, school counselor, or anyone you wish to see it.

The report cannot ethically be shared without your permission. (A sample release of information form is included on page 180.) You determine to whom you want the report released and why: You might want your psychotherapist to know so your ADD can be taken into account. You may wish to consult your family doctor about a medication trial. Perhaps you want your boss to work with you to maximize your work environment in order to improve your concentration; or, you might want your school professors to allow you extra time or a quiet place to take an exam. Finally, in many states, ADD is considered a disability that falls under the auspices of the state Rehabilitation Commission which could qualify you for retraining to do work that fits you better.

A Typical Report of an Adult with ADD

◀ Presenting Concern

Joe Smith, age thirty-three, married and father of a three-month-old son, requested an assessment for adult ADD because of job related difficulties. He complained of problems concentrating on sales reports, due weekly, that took him three times longer to complete than his fellow workers. He reported getting distracted by office noise, clutter on his desk and an inability to remain seated for the sixty to ninety minutes required to complete them. He also reported concern over his temper that flares anytime he feels someone is taking advantage of him. He reacts to slight, unintentional occurrences such as traffic errors by others and his wife's expectations that he be able to follow through on household chores.

◀ School History

Joe was repeatedly chastised in school for having difficulty completing assignments and for not staying on task. His IQ was consistently reported to be above average. He never worked up to potential. He disliked school and found great difficulty staying in his seat.

◀ Family History

Joe spoke caringly about his parents but got along better with his father than his mother who he described as having a temper like his. His father was easygoing and much easier for him to relate to. He and his mother would get into "spats," walk off from each other and five minutes later have forgotten the whole thing. His mother did many things in excess: eating, buying things on sale, and taking on volunteer jobs that she could not maintain control of. Many a project necessitated pulling all night duty, the night before it was due in order to achieve completion. But she was a creative person who had a heart of gold and he loved her very much. He had one sister who got real good grades and was calm, cool, and collected just like his dad. He and his sister have come to appreciate each other but he has always felt inferior and used to wish he could be like her to get the approval she received. He feels lucky that his parents let him spend summers with his grandparents where he could be outside most of the time, running free and doing physical work.

◀ Personal Life

Joe loves being on the go, is amiable except when his temper gets the best of him. He always wanted to be a vet because he loves animals so much but never seemed able to pull the grades required. He knew he was bright enough but just couldn't settle down. He loves music and watches a lot of TV. These both help him settle down.

When Joe was in high school he reports he drank too much but quit after a DWI scared him when he was twenty. He fears he could become addicted to alcohol easily. The only drug he experimented with was speed which he reported made him better able to focus on projects, but the side effects concerned him so he quit after a few months at age 18. Instead he drank. It didn't help his focusing but made him feel better temporarily from all the stress and fears of trying to get his life together.

Joe loves cars and wants to race them. He says the thrill makes him feel great. He's trying to save his money now so that he can become more involved in racing as a hobby. He dreams of "being someone" someday. He wants his son to be proud of him.

◀ Physical History

Joe was a full-term baby who suffered colic from about two to six months of age. He has a history of allergies to both airborne _____, some foods, and cats and dogs. (He does own pets but they mostly stay outside.) There is no history of head trauma, serious infectious illnesses, or seizures. Generally his health has been and is good with his last physical two years ago. He did have a broken arm as a child from falling off a roof at age ten, as well as several severe ligament sprains from trying to climb trees and cliffs and from various and sundry other impulsive physical activities.

◀ Job and Career History

When Joe couldn't make the grades to become a vet he tried several different jobs. He was happiest when he was around people and had the freedom to come and go as he pleased. He simply could not stand to sit behind a desk all day. He likes sales, but hates the paper work. No matter how hard he tries, he can't stay focused on completing it. He intends to, tries to motivate himself, resolves every Friday to do better, and continually fails to achieve his goals. When it comes to making a sale, though, he's quite successful.

Mostly he has gotten along well with his bosses. The exceptions occurred when he was either yelled at and shamed in an attempt to get him to do something, rather than being asked, or when he had an excitable boss who continually changed his mind. (Though Joe likes variety and new things, he likes to be the one who does the changing. It confuses him when changes happen to him.) Joe reports functioning best when there is a regular, simple structure for him to work within that is not too demanding, has freedom but regularity.

◀ Spouse Interview

Joe's wife Anita reported that he tends to promise more than he can produce. She doesn't feel he intends to let her down, but he just gets distracted. Basically they have a loving marriage and both adore their baby, who was planned. She laughed that the hardest thing about being married to Joe was that he wanted to have the ceiling fan in their bedroom on winter and summer and admitted that he sleeps better when it is on than not. He is restless at night and at times flails out in his sleep. She's learned to duck pretty well. Fortunately they both have a sense of humor and good communication. She says Joe is never still for long, moving from one activity to another in the house. Sometimes they'll be in the middle of conversation and he'll just get up and leave . . . not angrily, but he just goes into another room. If she follows him, he's very willing to continue the conversation, until he again moves to some other place. Usually he has gone to attend to some project or activity that he happened to think of while they were talking. At the movies, he drums his fingers and bounces his foot and often gets up at least once to get a drink or move around. In Sunday school, he is most comfortable sitting in the back of the room so he can get up during the discussion. She often notices him leaning against the doorway listening attentively. It's not that he isn't interested in the subject, he just can't sit still.

Joe's temper bothers her some, but she's learned that he gets over it quickly so she is less bothered than when they got married. Usually he reacts when he feels someone is blaming him for something or intruding in his space. She hopes he can get some help because she feels he is a real bright guy with a lot of potential if he can just pay attention.

◀ Observation

During the interview, Joe attended well the first ten minutes. Then he became restless, asked to get a drink of water after about twenty minutes and it was necessary to break the ninety-minute interview into several segments. Throughout the interview he jiggled his feet, drummed his fingers, and shifted his weight. He obviously is a well socialized, polite man who is cognizant of appropriate behavior and wants to cooperate.

Emotionally, Joe recalled many incidents in school when he was misunderstood and accused of not trying, when in reality he tried very hard. He said he always wanted to do better than he could do. He feels bad that he "caused his parents so much trouble." He never meant to. Now he's worried that he will fail his family because it's just so hard for him to get everything done that needs to be done. There is no indication

177

that he doesn't want to do these things. He just keeps losing his attention.

◀ Summary

Joe Smith is a thirty-three-year-old married father of one who demonstrates numerous aspects of Attention Deficit Disorder. There is no indication that other physical or emotional abnormalities are present to account for his behavior. Joe can be expected to benefit from training to structure his life job and home projects. His wife will benefit from training to help her understand his needs and they can make tradeoffs to maximize each of their skills.

At work, record-keeping needs to be simplified for him. In addition, he may be able to track the records in a more beneficial manner during the week and his wife, in lieu of a secretary, may be able to help him complete the necessary paper work in a more timely manner. He, in turn, is willing to take on one of her jobs for which he is more suited.

It has been recommended that Joe modify his diet with the help of a nutritionist. Particular attention needs to be paid to his tendency to consume candy, especially when he is frustrated doing paper work.

Joe is being referred for a medication assessment.

He is also being referred to a group to remediate the guilt and frustration he experienced growing up because of his ADD.

Follow-up is recommended at three months.

Model Letter
to a Physician

▼

To Whom It May Concern:

Your patient, _____, has contacted the Dr. Lynn Weiss Center, Inc. requesting an evaluation for Attention Deficit Disorder, Residual Type. We have done an initial assessment using the enclosed evaluation tool and have found that he/she meets the criteria for ADD-RT (314.80) in the DSM III (Undifferentiated Attention Deficit Disorder, 314.00 in the DSM III—R).

We have recommended a medical evaluation with you for further assessment. In conjunction with the medical referral, we are offering counseling to deal with the psychosocial aspects of ADD.

The research indicates that for some ADD adults, medication can be of significant benefit. We feel there is a need to address this problem both from a medical and psychological perspective. We hope you will assist us in further assessing this patient.

Enclosed is some information to further familiarize you with this topic. After the medical evaluation is complete, we will provide the necessary psychotherapeutic follow-up care. We look forward to working with you in the future and hope that you will let us know if there are any other adult patients who might benefit from psychosocial treatment for ADD.

Sincerely yours,
Lynn Weiss, Ph.D.

Sample Permission
To Obtain and
Release Information

▼

I hereby grant permission to _____ to request and obtain reports of psychological and psychiatric evaluations and/or medical, school, social, and/or other appropriate records pertaining to:

_____   _____
(Name)   (Birthdate)

Permission is also granted for _____ to share findings, reports, and/or other information that might be helpful in the understanding and treatment of this client with other professional staff of the Dr. Lynn Weiss Center, Inc. and insurance companies if requested for processing your claim.

The signer recognizes and agrees that a copy of this form is acceptable and binding and will serve as an original in any instance.

_____   _____
(Date)   (Name)

                                                _____
                                                (Relationship to Client)

180

Medication and Attention Deficit Disorder in Adults

▼

◀ Interview with Dr. Judy Cook

When it comes to medication of adults with Attention Deficit Disorder, I have run into what seems like a lack of agreement between professionals, yielding confusion and misinformation. So, I decided to talk with a professional whom I respect about medication and Attention Deficit Disorder in adults.

Dr. Judy Cook received her medical degree from The University of Texas in San Antonio Medical School. She did her pathology residency at The University of Texas Health Science Center in Dallas and her psychiatric residency at The University of Texas at San Antonio Health Science Center. She has merged her interests to become a neuropsychiatrist. Her private practice is in Dallas, Texas, where she is also the Director of Brainmapping Associates.

LYNN WEISS: When we talk about the medication of Attention Deficit Disorder in adults, what is the most important thing that goes through your head?

DR. JUDY COOK: The first thing is a very good diagnostic workup that makes sure we are dealing with ADD and not something else driving the difficulty in paying attention. It's important to rule out other things like environmental stress, agitated depression, and seizure disorders.

Once ADD has become the diagnosis to be treated, then it is a matter of trial and error regarding medication.

181

Ritalin is a medication that has been used for a long, long time. Research has shown that this stimulant drug works with people with ADD because it helps to focus their attention and concentrating mechanism. If it is not the right drug, then it will make the person more hyper rather than less. If it is the right drug, then it ought to be possible to establish a dose level that the person will be able to stay on without having to continually increase the dose. The person should get a pretty consistent result from it.

Then I worry about the additional problems: is it going to disturb sleep, is it going to interfere with growth in children, is it going to interfere with appetite. That's why with children you have weekend and summer vacations from the drug to see whether their nervous system is going to allow them to compensate and no longer need the medication. In addition it allows sleep, growth, and appetite to normalize.

With an adult you will want to watch for similar problems and if you have them, you will want to try another drug. Alternative drugs to look at are Cylert or one of the tricyclic antidepressants, usually Imipramine or Desiprimine. Cylert is minimal in terms of side effects or problems. Most people tolerate that pretty well. Like all drugs, it works well in some and doesn't in some.

LW: Sounds like a real guessing game!

JC: It's like any number of other things in psychiatry. Everybody's chemistry is different. You give twenty people the same dose of a drug and you get twenty different responses. That's why it's rather distressing when people want to go out and trade drugs, "Gee, this works great for me, try some." It can be dangerous.

The tricyclic antidepressants are used in a wide range of dosages from tiny of 10 mg per day to levels comparable for the treatment of depression, at 150 mg per day. Some standard side effects are some sedation, some dry mouth, occasionally some constipation, initially feeling kind of tired and sluggish.

182

Those side effects usually clear up over time as the body gets adjusted to it.

This is the main cadre of drugs used to treat ADD. Of course there are the behavior treatments that must go hand in hand with the biochemical treatment.

LW: What are some guidelines for a person working with a physician to get accustomed to medication for ADD?

JC: A person needs to be followed by a physician when on any kind of medication. Initially it's wise to see the doctor once every week or two to make sure things are going okay. We're talking about a 15-minute visit. Sometimes I'll give people guidelines on how to increase medication over time. If I don't give the person those guidelines, I expect the person to stay at the dose I put him on until the next visit, not up and not down, unless we talk about it. The patient does not know what the side effects of changing the dosage might be and so might put himself in a toxic range or cause a withdrawal problem.

If a patient is having a side effect and it's a scary one—passing out, break out in a rash, severe stomach pain, a seizure—he should stop the medication first and call the doctor second. Short of major things, call the doctor and talk with him to see if its a side effect of the medication.

Some drugs work slowly, others affect the person quickly. As a general rule the antidepressants are very slow to build up to the amount in the body that is going to be effective; four to six weeks. In contrast, Ritalin works pretty rapidly and wears off rapidly. It has a short half-life. Yet, you will tend to get an accrual of a little more benefit over time than at first. It may not seem that way because one of the peculiar aspects of the human animal is that we forget how bad we felt when we get to feeling better.

LW: In this day and age there is a lot of drug education; it teaches us that we don't want our loved ones doped up. Would you comment?

JC: This question always stirs up ambivalent feelings in me. I'm basically one of those people who will treat people with no medications at all if possible. I think prescription drugs should be used carefully. Rather than just trying to live better chemically, solving the underlying problem is important. On the other hand, if you need the drug, *take it.* If a drug is what it takes to bring your physiology into normal range, don't just sit there and worry about being a doper.

LW: Talk about the difference between masking a symptom with medication and correcting or adding something when the body isn't working right.

JC: Sometimes you are doing some of both. At times you're goosing the biochemical system in order to produce or inhibit a particular chemical. You don't, in these situations, cure the disease any more than you cure diabetes by controlling the symptoms. Very often you have to stay on the drug forever because you aren't going to cure the disease. Anxiety is a symptom you can mask with an anxiety medication. Psychotherapy, however, gives you the skills to really overcome the problem and cure it.

LW: Do you ever cure ADD?

JC: (Laugh) I don't think you cure it. I think that there are a cluster of people who do outgrow it. At puberty all the rules change. Your neurology and neurophysiology continues to modify. Some people's brains will correct the problem; others won't.

LW: Some people learn good socialization, good behavioral skills, and it looks like they don't have ADD any longer, but it still comes out in subtle forms. The person may be able to control his behavior so well that he has mastery of the ADD most of the time, but it pops out here and there.

JC: Are there particular predictable times you're aware of?

LW: Tiredness and anytime there is change . . . because one of the ways the person may control it is by patterning his life,

184

having himself on a schedule . . . but let the schedule be disrupted and you see the bouncing around.

JC: One thing worth trying with someone like that, who is sophisticated enough that you can trust what they do with their medication, is to let them have some of the medication and say, "Use it at those times when you know the situation is such that it is likely to put you out of balance." This works in times when the system is overloaded. You can learn all the skills of control, but sometimes even the skills are going to get overwhelmed.

LW: The next issue is addiction to the drugs used in treating ADD.

JC: Ritalin is the one drug with which we worry about addiction. Interestingly, in people who are responsive to Ritalin, once they get on the correct dosage they don't tend to use more and more. Their bodies don't begin craving more, and they don't begin to psychologically crave it.

When you have someone who has a chemically dependent personality, the person will continue to use more and more and more Ritalin and that becomes a warning sign. That's the time to reassess the situation, checking to see if, indeed, the person has ADD or if there is some other problem or some other medication that you ought to use.

LW: That does not tend to come up with Cylert or the tricyclic antidepressants?

JC: No, those drugs just do not tend to create those kinds of cravings.

LW: Which leads to the next issue. I had a patient who had been a drug and alcohol abuser. She had been in a solid recovery program for two and a half years and had gained a lot of skills. I diagnosed ADD after all of the other things were cleared away. She needed medication, but both of us were very protective of her sobriety. A physician put her on Tofranil.

JC: Yes, that's a case in which you would want to use Cylert or a tricyclic antidepressant, which is what Tofranil is.

LW: Are there other times besides with addiction when the use of some drugs for ADD are contraindicated?

JC: If someone has a seizure disorder, you want to be very careful so you don't worsen their seizure problem. A good history is the most important thing you do in these cases. If a doctor doesn't do that, then change doctors.

LW: What about the use of any of the drugs mentioned and the use of alcohol?

JC: I recommend to people who are on any kind of a mood-altering drug that they really modify their alcohol intake and that they avoid street drugs. There is very often a compounding effect. You tend to be vulnerable to the effects of the drugs and they tend to be multiplicative rather than additive. Be careful!

LW: One youngster, age seven, was put on Ritalin for several months. It worked well for him. Another thirteen-year-old had the same results and was on it for three and a half years. Both are no longer taking Ritalin. It looks like behavioral patterns they were able to establish with the help of the medication have held. Trying to get the behavior patterns into place without the medication was virtually impossible. Talk about this kind of use of medication.

JC: To me, this is the optimal use of medication. If you can use the medication to put the person in such a place that they can work through things in psychotherapy, very often you can wean them off of the medication and they will cope. Some people will be able to totally come off the medication, some will need it on an *ad lib* basis, and some will always need the medication plus the benefits they got out of psychotherapy. It's highly variable.

LW: Comment on the use of brainmapping and ADD.

JC: Brainmapping is a very nice use of modern technology, the marriage of computers and EEG (Electroencephalograph). It measures how the brain functions as opposed to a picture of what it looks like anatomically. It tells us how the brain works. It can really show us, particularly when we are doing an early evaluation, whether there is something else going on. Is there another problem that is impairing learning and concentration that needs to be solved? If a child has learning disabilities and sees that he is not learning with his peers, he will get upset and act out. If you help solve the learning disability problem, or even just help him know he's an okay person even though he has a learning disability, you may do a lot to calm behavior.

I saw one kid who was making excellent grades but he was so hyperactive they were ready to kick him out of school. They wanted to blame the family. Well, this kid had a seizure disorder and when we put him on a seizure medicine his hyperactivity went away. He'd been tried on ADD medication and it hadn't done the job because his problem had been misdiagnosed.

That's one of the nice things about this new technology. I like to see it used early on in the course of working someone up because in the long term it's cost effective both financially and emotionally to make the best diagnosis the first time. This way it is not necessary to go through a lot of trial and error in medication.

Unfortunately I see a lot of patients who are medicated by trial and error. And too often the person has been given several medications at the same time. That's not good medicine and not good practice.

LW: How do you as a physician feel about a person wanting to take part in diagnosing their condition?

JC: I'm in favor of every patient being as informed and knowledgeable as they can about their illness. But, that means more than reading one article. I try to educate them about their problem and their medication and then I encourage them to go on and read more. I think they should be very tuned into the management of their illness and I think it's good to be tuned into their symptoms. But, they need to back off and realize they are not physicians. A team effort means you need to give the doctor some credit for having some sense, just as the doctor needs to give the patient some credit for having some sense. Optimum care really involves good team work.

LW: So, if a patient has a doctor who won't talk about the patient's condition and wants to be completely in charge with the patient passively accepting . . .

JC: My idea on that is that the patient should run frantically and find someone else. There are patients who want to be babied and taken care of and have the doctor pamper them and that's why some doctors are still that way. It's certainly easier from the doctor's standpoint than to have to argue with and educate the patient. You can treat a lot more patients. But I strongly encourage patients to become educated about their disease so that they can form a partnership with the doctor.

LW: Anything else you want to say?

JC: I think with ADD and other medical problems, you really need to be careful to look for doctors and other treatment people who are legitimate and are looking out for your best interests. You should be wary of doctors who try to milk you as a money machine, try to do excessive treatment, or try to cut you off from family.

LW: All doctors can legally prescribe medication. You are a psychiatrist, so you have special training in certain kinds of medications. What kinds of doctors are likely to know the pharmacology associated with ADD? And what about the use of a family doctor by people who don't have specialists available?

JC: It is a rare family doctor who will know about ADD. Pediatricians do a lot of treating of ADD. Some are knowledgeable and some are not.

188

LW: My experience has been that they will not talk to an adult about ADD.

JC: Right. There are many psychiatrists who are not that knowledgeable about ADD in adults. Child and adolescent psychiatrists are probably the most knowledgeable because that's one of the things they see a lot of. Part of the rule of thumb is to look for someone who has had some experience in it. Try to find someone else who has had the disorder and had good luck with a doctor treating it. Know that there will be doctors out there who have never treated it, don't know anything about it, haven't read about it, and yet are willing to prescribe. And, they may prescribe the wrong things.

I don't try to go around prescribing cardiac medications, though I may be more knowledgeable than the average psychiatrist. Unfortunately, there's a real tendency for doctors to not feel that way about psychiatric medication. It's almost like every doctor out there thinks he knows how to be a psychiatrist, or at least how to write a prescription for Valium, an antidepressant, or a little of this or that. In fact, he knows about as much about prescribing psychiatric medication as I do about doing open heart surgery. Be sure your doctor recognizes his boundaries.

LW: If a person is living in an area where there are limitations in finding specialists, what recommendations do you have in terms of treatment.

JC: Sometimes you can work out something where you have a doctor from a larger metropolitan area evaluate you and establish the treatment and then communicate with your local GP in terms of follow-up and what needs to be done.

Small area doctors tend to be one of two kinds: either very good or very bad, and usually very little in between. If you are getting treatment and things are not getting better, think about getting treatment in a larger metropolitan area.

Attention Deficit Disorder in Adults Workshop

▼

A three- to four-hour public workshop can be an invaluable community, college, or business tool to assist with initial identification of Attention Deficit Disorder in adults. There is a high level of accurate self referral from this group of people.

At least two breaks are advisable, as well as an opportunity for people to move about, stretch, listen to a speaker for a while, then fill out the checklist and have small group discussions. Variability in format is essential.

I. Introduction and Overview for the Day

II. Content

    a. Screening checklist—to be filled out by each participant with regard to self or another

    b. What Attention Deficit Disorder is—symptoms

    c. More complete assessment procedures

    d. Diagnostic criterion and complications, dual diagnosis

    e. Treatment options

    f. Medication

    g. Resources in local area

h.   Success cases

i.   Living with ADD—special problems from the point of view of the significant other

III.   Questions and Answers

Though questions and answers will be entertained throughout the workshop, they will be restricted to items of clarification since much of the material will be covered automatically. This section will be open for remaining questions and specific, personal questions.

IV.   Handouts will include:

a.   Checklist to be filled out

b.   A list of symptoms

c.   A list of references

d.   A list of local and national resources

Running an ADD Group

▼

*I*n the education and treat-
ment of adults with Attention Deficit Disorder, I have discovered that a fairly short group meeting/class/session works
the best. Similarly, it needs to run for a limited time period to
hold the interest of the participants. This group is led by
people who have a solid, practical, working knowledge of
ADD in adults and good group leadership skills. This can be
either a professional or a trained lay person. This group is
designed differently from a support group in terms of intent
and format.

Time: Four weeks
One and one half hours in length

Format: Get acquainted time followed by presentation
of information and group discussion with
personal examples. Then questions and answers
and special needs.

Leadership: The group can be led by a mental health
clinician, educator, or group leader trained in
the area of Attention Deficit Disorder in adults.
Peer facilitators can serve effectively as
co-leaders to keep the leaders on track. They
have special capabilities since they have been
there. Training groups for professionals are
available in local areas while the workshops are
running.

Week 1:   Add fifteen to thirty minutes for registration, refreshments, and get acquainted time

    a.   What it's like to have ADD. Presentation by peer leader is especially effective here.

    b.   Input by participants as they air their concerns about having discovered they have ADD. Personal stories are much in order here.

    c.   Participants list special problems they are facing on paper so leaders can be sure to incorporate solutions into future meetings.

    d.   A brief discussion of medication use often arises during this first meeting and referrals can be made for medication assessment.

Week 2:   Handling feelings

    a.   Present and past feelings need to be elicited from the participants.

    b.   Grief work is essential in helping people with ADD grieve for the losses incurred because of the condition.

    c.   Trauma reduction using imagery techniques is beneficial. If a trained professional is not available to implement this aspect, referrals can be made for those people requiring it. All participants can benefit, however, from the work in the group setting.

    d.   A stress reduction/relaxation technique needs to be taught.

Week 3:   Organizational management skills

    a.   Each participant needs to bring home and work examples of time management problems. Schedules are worked up and scheduling structures developed as date books and charts.

193

b. Ways to break up time are shared so that the person is more "in control."

c. Permission is given for each participant to do whatever is necessary timewise in order to be successful. This includes leaving things to the last moment, working with the TV on, etc.

d. Spatial management changes are developed including the use of work carrels and other ways to break up space for more effective concentration.

e. Brainstorming is used to assist individuals to develop solutions to complicated situations. A letter may be developed for an ADD person to take to his or her boss or manager requesting special work arrangements. (A boost in productivity is quite appealing to many employers, particularly if it is only a matter of a fairly minor adjustment that makes the difference.)

Week 4:   Interpersonal relations

a. Participants share specific problems they are confronted with in their relationships.

b. Communications training is presented and practiced to help ADD people get their needs met and in turn meet the needs of those with whom they interface.

c. Temper control and techniques to defuse "hot" situations are taught.

d. Negotiation skills are outlined and practiced.

e. This final week ends with an appraisal of the question, "Who am I if I am in charge of my life and in control of my ADD?"

An optional fifth week may be added for couples to work on personal issues. The ADD person is accompanied by his or her spouse or special friend.

Week 5:   Living with an ADD person

a.   Communication skills are taught and practiced.

b.   Negotiation skills are taught and practiced.

c.   Grief recovery and burying the hatchet
work is accomplished.

d.   Sexual communication and shared problems and pleasures are discussed and plans
made to modify or change existing prac-
tices. Agreements are verbalized to put
these into practice. Escape clauses are
woven into the plans with mutual respect
taking precedence.

Setting Up an ADD Support Group

▼

A support group is a group of people who share a common problem and voluntarily come together for emotional support, information sharing (from those who are further down the road), resources, and problem solving.

You enter the group alone—you come out knowing you're not alone.

Support groups have the following characteristics:

Makeup: People who have a common problem they've not been trained to handle. Traditionally, support groups do not have a professional leader, though there may be an advisor. Specialists may be called in from time to time as speakers.

Desire: The individuals have a desire to solve or learn to live more effectively with their problem.

Scheduling: They tend to meet on a regular, predictable basis.

Politics: No one's vested interests are served by the group. It is not a way for one person to build business or in any way take advantage of the members. The group is organized for the purpose of assisting its members with the specific, identified problem.

To Start A Group:

◀ Check with your community's local clearing house to see if there is already one started, such as:

> The Mental Health Association

> An Information and Referral Service

or a national organization such as:

> The National ADD in Adults Support Group

◀ Volunteer to serve as a contact person for others to call for information about a new group. Make a list of callers and get a couple of helpers. Find a place and set a date for the first meeting. Develop a network to get information out about the beginning group. Let the media and professionals know as they will make good referral sources.

◀ Meet with your local support group clearing house representative to get advise about starting and maintaining your support group.

◀ Consult a guide to support groups. An excellent resource is:

> *Helping You Helps Me: A Guide Book For Self-Help Groups*, by Karen Hill. Canadian Council on Social Development, 1987. Available from:

>> Canadian Council of Social Development, Publications,
>> 55 Parkdale Avenue
>> Ottawa, Ontario
>> K1Y 4G1
>> (613)728-1865a

You'll need to consider issues including:

◀ Generating membership

◀ Mutual partnership of the support group and professionals

◀ Maintenance

>   —balancing individual and group needs
>
>   —leadership and control
>
>   —agenda issues—support, education, activism, etc.
>
>   —communication
>
>   —confidentiality

Support groups can be wonderful. They can also get out of control and do damage to participants unless they are responsibly managed. If you become involved in a group that makes you feel worse rather than appreciably better, beware and look for another group or start your own. Don't hesitate to consult with a professional who is accustomed to dealing with self-help groups.

Organizations that Help Adults with ADD

▼

ADDult Support Network
c/o Mary Jane Johnson, Organizer
2620 Ivy Place
Toledo, Ohio 43613

> The primary focus of this organization is to provide a national network for all adult ADD support groups and adult ADD individuals.

Support materials available:

◀ Pen Pal listing to allow ADD adults to correspond with other ADD adults. ($2.00/yr.)

◀ ADDult Information Packet: Includes several personal stories and article reprints. ($3.00)

◀ ADDult News (quarterly newsletter): Personal stories, tips, news, open forum. ($8.00/yr.)

◀ *INSIDE ADD—By an Adult Who Has Been There,* by Susan Alfultis. A 75-page spiral book that includes her personal story, journal entries, poems, and artwork. ($16.00)

◀ *ADD—A Lifetime Challenge: Lifestories of Adults with Attention Deficit Disorder.* Each chapter has been written by a different ADD adult (spiral-bound, $12.95).

◀ ADDA (Attention Deficit Disorder Association)

ADDA was formed to unify and encourage ADD support organizations and to serve as a voice of national advocacy for ADD-affected individuals in matters related to health and education. The Founders of ADDA came together in 1988 to work toward common goals:

◀ To represent and respond to the needs and concerns of existing ADD support groups

◀ To facilitate the establishment of independent ADD support groups where needed and to assist individuals in underserved areas

◀ To establish a public policy agenda to address statements and claims made about Attention Deficit Disorder through the media

◀ To help anyone wanting to start a group, ADDA is willing to exchange information and offer assistance. Materials are currently being formulated to assist groups in getting started.

Contact: Challenge Newsletter
            c/o Jean Harrison
            P.O. Box 2001
            West Newbury, Massachusetts 01985
            (508) 462-0495

Cost: $50.00 for support group
            $25.00 for individuals

ANE (Adult Network Exchange)
P.O. Box 1701
Ann Arbor, Michigan 48106

The group was formed to provide a network link for and between the organizations serving adults. In May 1993, they co-sponsored, with

200

the Adult Support Network, the first annual conference focusing on adult issues. Annual conferences will be presented. This national liaison will share information to increase ADD literacy among individuals and professionals associated with the various organizations.

Contact: (313) 426-1659

Cost: none

CHADD
499 NW 70th Avenue, Suite 308
Plantation, Florida 33317

A support group for parents whose children have ADD disorders, adults with ADD, and professionals who have an interest in Attention Deficit Disorders. The publications and activities often contain information about adults. CHADD sponsors a national conference and interrelates with national organizations forming coalitions that work for the benefit of children and adults with ADD.

Contact: (305) 587-3700

Cost: Individual, $30.00/year
             Professional, $60.00
             International, $100.00 (outside U.S. and Canada)
             Organizational, $150.00

Support materials available:

CHADDER is published two times per year in journal/magazine format containing articles written by experts.

CHADDer Box, published monthly (except for summers), is a member's newsletter.

201

Learning Disabilities Association of America
c/o Jean Peterson, Executive Director
4156 Library Road
Pittsburgh, Pennsylvania 15234
(412) 341-1515

Information/Resources

▼

*T*he following list is not meant to be inclusive nor should it be taken as a recommendation of professional skills.

◀ Articles in Professional Journals

"Attention Deficit Disorders Persisting in Adulthood: A Review." *Comprehensive Psychiatry,* July–August 1982. Henry Amada and Patrick J. Lustman.

"Stimulant Medications in Adults with Attention Deficit Disorder." *Canadian Journal of Psychiatry,* August 1984. Martin Gautheir.

"Long Term Outcome of Hyperactive Children." *Annual Progress in Child Psychiatry and Child Development,* 1984. Lily Hectman and Gabrielle Weiss.

"Dysthymia and Attention Deficit Disorder in Adults." *American Journal of Psychiatry,* January 1982. Jefferey Mattes.

"The Diagnosis and Treatment of ADD, RT." *Psychiatric Annals,* January 1986. David Woods.

"Attention Deficit Disorder in Adults." *Psychiatric Annals,* January 1986. Steven H. Klee, Barry D. Garfinkel, and Hortense Beauchesne.

"Computerized EEG Can Identify Attention Deficit Disorder." *Clinical Psychiatry News,* August 1987. Robert H. Gerner.

◀ Books

Hyperactive Children Grown Up by Lily Hechtman and Gabrielle Weiss, The Guilford Press, 1986.

◀ Newsletters and Handouts

ADDendum (for adult sufferers of ADD)
c/o CPS
5041-A Back Lick Road
Annadale, VA 22003
(914) 278-3022
Editor: Paul Jaffe, Legal Editor: Peter Latham, Esq.

ADDult News
2620 Ivy Place
Toledo, OH 43613

ADD Vantage
P.O. Box 29972
Thornton, CO 80229

ADDvisor
Attention Deficit Resource Center
P.O. Box 71223
Marietta, GA 30007-1223
Voice mail: (800) 537-3784

Resource People
with an Interest
in ADD in Adults
and Support Groups

▼

*T*hanks to Paul Jaffe, Addendum
*Newsletter editor, and Jim Reisinger, Ann Arbor, Michigan support
group, for their invaluable assistance in compiling these resources.*

◀ Alabama

Support Groups

Birmingham
Rev. John Larsen, (205) 823-5910

◀ Arizona

Robert Gurnee
7150 East Camelback Road, Suite 300
Scottsdale, AZ 85251
(602) 423-7770

Support Groups

Phoenix Area/Scottsdale
Robert Gurnee, (602) 423-7770

Western Yavapai County/Chino Valley
Marcia Brehmer, (602) 636-5160

◀ California

Joan Andrews
Coastline Counseling
1200 Quail Street, Suite 105
Newport Beach, CA 92660-2706
(714) 476-0991

Joanne (Jody) Ross
P.O. Box 20184
Castro Valley, CA 94546
(510) 803-1068
Available to anyone interested in ADD in adults.

Walid O. Shekim, M.D.
UCLA Neuropsychiatric Institute and Hospital
300 UCLA Medical Plaza, Rm. 1414
Los Angeles, CA 90024-6967
(213) 825-6554
Available to anyone interested in ADD in adults.

Melissa Thomasson, Ph.D.
125 Baker Street, Suite 263 East
Costa Mesa, CA 92626
(714) 545-7038
Available to anyone interested in ADD in adults.

Support Groups

Bay Area/Contra Costa County
Pat Churchill, (415) 825-4938
Rita Wilson, (510) 524-3953

Long Beach
Patreen Bauer, Sue Griffith, (310) 493-1496

Mid-Peninsula/Palo Alto
Kitty Petty, (415) 329-9443

Orange County/Newport Beach
Joan Andrews, (714) 476-0991

Sacramento Area/Roseville
Dr. Milton Lucius, (916) 933-5217

Santa Clara County/San Jose
Karen Neale, (408) 395-1348

◀ Colorado

Ralph Myers
P.O. Box 29972
Thornton, CO 80229-0972
(303) 287-6944
Available to anyone interested in ADD in adults.

Support Groups

Boulder
Andrea Scott, (303) 440-9193

Denver
Don Lambert, (303) 424-5272

Denver Metro Area East/Aurora
Jim Dameron, (303) 693-9715

Denver Metro Area North/Adams County
Pamela Stone, (303) 277-1059

Front Range/Adams County
Ralph Myers (303) 287-6944,
(303) 821-2428 (pager)

Northern Colorado/Fort Collins
Lou Hartmeister, (303) 221-1835
Maxine Jarvis, (303) 223-1338

◀ Connecticut

Support Groups

Hartford Area/West Hartford
Michael Kissane, (203) 277-8669
Joel Shusman, (203) 236-0001

North Branford
Sean Murphy, (203) 483-7238

Southeast Connecticut/East Hampton
Cathy Ziegler, (203) 267-6807

◀ Florida

Support Groups

Broward County/Plantation
Diana Kennedy, (305) 726-4590

Volusia and Seminole Counties/Deltona
Rebecca Burleson, (904) 532-5651

◀ Georgia

Edna D. Copeland, Ph.D.
Southeastern Psychological Institute
P.O. Box 12389
Atlanta, GA 30355-2389
(404) 256-4333
Available to anyone interested in ADD in adults.

Support Groups

Atlanta
Larry Melear, (404) 971-4763

Columbus
Amy Darby, (706) 563-7419

◀ Illinois

Support Groups

Central Illinois/Bloomington
Ron Ropp, (309) 829-0751

Chicago Area/Rolling Meadows
Becky Booth, (708) 303-1189

◀ Indiana

Support Groups

Northwest Indiana/Gary Area/Valparaiso
Bill Hayes, (219) 465-1655

Northwest Indiana/Portage
Teresa Gross, (219) 465-0447
David Shultz, (219) 232-6690

◀ Kansas

Support Groups

Greater Kansas City Area/Overland Park
Dr. Avner Stern, (913) 469-6510

◀ Maine

Support Groups

Southern Maine/Lewiston
Lindy Botto, (207) 883-2528

◀ Maryland

Dr. Maureen Donnelly
5225 Pooks Hill Road
Bethesda, MD 20814
(301) 564-6083

Kathleen Nadeau, Ph.D.
4400 East-West Highway, Suite 816
Bethesda, MD 20814
(301) 718-8114
Available to anyone interested in ADD in adults.

Support Groups

Montgomery County/Silver Spring
Dr. Kathleen Nadeau, (301) 718-8114

◀ Massachusetts

Ned Hallowell, M.D.
328 Broadway
Cambridge, MA 02139
(617) 547-6952
Available to anyone interested in ADD in adults.

Linda Harrison
P.O. Box 2256
Peabody, MA 01960
(508) 535-3131
Available to anyone interested in ADD in adults.

Walter Harrison, M.D.
34 Lynnfield Street
Lynn, MA 01904
(617) 596-2255
Available to professionals concerned about ADD.

Alex Taubman
140 Bay St. Rd.
Box # 5043
Boston, MA 02215
(617) 352-7196
Available to anyone interested in ADD in adults.

Support Groups

Boston Area/Boston, Weston
John Moir, (603) 881-5540

Cape Cod/West Barnstable
John Welles, (508) 428-2102

North Shore/Lynn
(an adult section of the Lynn parents' group)
Linda Harrison, (505) 535-3131

South Shore/Plymouth
Linda Greenwood, (508) 747-2179

210

◀ Michigan

Support Groups

Ann Arbor
Jim Reisinger, (313) 426-1659

Detroit Area North/Troy
Kathleen Van Howe, (313) 939-1112
Dawn Orton, (313) 726-9368

Detroit Area West/Novi
Fred Michaelson, (313) 855-8585, (313) 348-2656

◀ Minnesota

Support Groups

Twin Cities Area/Minnetonka
William Ronan, (612) 933-3460

◀ New Hampshire

Sarah Brophy, Ph.D.
253 Pleasant Street
Concord, NH 03301
(603) 226-6121
Available to anyone interested in ADD in adults.

Support Groups

Central New Hampshire/Concord
Dr. Sarah Brophy, (603) 226-6121

◀ New Jersey

Support Groups

Monmouth and Ocean Counties/Long Branch
Dr. Robert LoPresti, (908) 842-4553
Phyllis Wolff, (908) 870-5053

◀ New Mexico

Robert Gurnee
801 Encino Place, Suite 314
Albuquerque, NM 87102
(505) 243-9600

◀ New York

Leopold Bellak, M.D.
22 Rockwood Drive
Larchmont, NY 10538
Available to professionals for consultation on ADD in adults.

Rachel G. Klein
NY State Psychiatric Institute
722 West 168th Street, Box 80
New York, NY 10032
Available to anyone interested in ADD in adults.

Support Groups

New York City/Manhattan
Paul Jaffe, (914) 278-3022

Rochester
Peter Meinhold, (716) 482-3002

Rockland County/Pomona
Rosemarie Bone, (914) 354-0200 x 3609

Westchester County/White Plains
Susan Salit, (914) 472-2935

◀ Ohio

Support Groups

Cincinnati
Kate Kelly, (513) 861-8519

Miami Valley/Xenia
Bettylou Huber, (513) 862-4573
Madge Jones, (513) 897-4380
Steve Ledingham, (513) 767-1207

Toledo
Jan, (409) 841-6603

◄ Oklahoma

Support Groups

Oklahoma City
Diana Mathia, (405) 722-1233

◄ Pennsylvania

Dr. Barbara Korzun
Attention Deficit Mastery
700 South Henderson Road, Suite 302A
King of Prussia, PA 19406
(215) 337-4552

Support Groups

Bucks County/Bensalem
Jeff Segal, (215) 639-9341
Carol Steiner, (215) 355-5908

Bucks & Montgomery Counties/Telford
Ginger Varley, (215) 723-8587

*Chester, Delaware, & Montgomery
Counties/Norristown*
Joan Kempton, (215) 565-8676
Dr. Richard Straub, (215) 469-6633

Lancaster County
Judy Mansfield, (717) 656-9515

Philadelphia/Center City
Harvey Kravetz, (215) 732-9541
Rose St. Julien, (215) 732-4639

Philadelphia/Main Line/Bryn Mawr
Jerry McCrone, (215) 647-8807

◀ **Texas**

Center for Adults with ADD
founded by Lynn Weiss, Ph.D.
2710 Oaklawn, Suite 210
Dallas, TX 75219
(214) 369-1104

Judy Cook, M.D.
(214) 233-9063
Available to professionals interested in ADD in adults.

Nancy Eisenberg
12345 Jones Road, Suite 101
Houston, TX 77070
(713) 469-0749

Jeff Glass, M.D.
7515 Greenville Avenue, Suite 806
Dallas, TX 75231
(214) 361-5156

Byron Kocen, M.D.
11111 Research #150
Austin, TX 78759
(512) 338-5150

Catherine Matchett, M.D.
230 Park Boulevard, Suite 106
Grapevine, TX 76051
(817) 481-9511

Tricia Raley, Ph.D.
200 West Highway 6, Suite 505
Waco, TX 76712
(817) 751-1550

Support Groups

Austin
Sue Satoff, (512) 477-5516

Dallas
Larry Steele, (817) 498-6842
Cindy Taylor, (817) 387-8039

Plano (ADD of Dallas Adult Chapter)
Leslie, (214) 596-6233

Houston
Karen Kasper, (713) 288-6758
Dale Robinson, (713) 721-0278

◀ Utah

Fred Reimherr, M.D.
Department of Psychiatry
University of Utah Medical Center
Salt Lake City, UT 84132
Available to anyone interested in ADD in adults.

◀ Vermont

Hans Huessy, M.D.
RR 2 Box 367
Jericho, VT 05465
(802) 899-5016
Available to anyone interested in ADD in adults.

◀ Virginia

Kathleen Nadeau, Ph.D.
5041-A Back Lick Road
Annadale, VA 22003
(703) 642-6697

215

Dr. Martin Stein
11200 Waples Mill Road, # 150
Fairfax, VA 22030
(703) 385-6111

Support Groups

Northern Virginia/Falls Church
Susan Biggs, (703) 642-6697

Peninsula/Newport News
Mark Jacob, (804) 874-7992

Southwest Virginia/Roanoke
Debra Maxey, (703) 387-2307

◀ Washington

Lisa F. Poast
1225 East Sunset Drive, Suite 640
Bellingham, WA 98226
(206) 647-6681
Available to anyone interested in ADD in adults.

Support Groups

Bellingham
Tom Melo, (206) 647-5523
Lisa Poast, (206) 647-6681

Seattle
Carol Lee Crabill, (206) 246-9752
Dr. Willis McNabb, (206) 609-3470

◀ Wisconsin

Paul Rembas
204 Wisconsin Avenue
Waukesha, WI 53186
(414) 542-6694
Available for anyone interested in ADD in adults.

Support Groups

Milwaukee Area/Waukesha
Paul Rembas, (414) 542-5445, 542-6694

Rock Valley/Janesville
Doug and Cathy Kitzman, (608) 870-6074

◀ U.S. Virgin Islands

Support Groups

St. Croix/Kingshill
Susan Miller, (809) 778-1431

◀ Canada

Support Groups

Ottawa
Marc Turcotte, (613) 234-3346